> * If you don't know how to draft an EVAL or a FITREP,
> You don't know how to read one--your own included.
>
> * The more you use these writing guides, the greater your
> ability to understand and write EVALS and FITREPS

ENLISTED EVAL AND OFFICER FITREP WRITING GUIDE

This 300+ page Writing Guide is ideally suited for the person who:

*Is new to the art of writing (and understanding) Evals and Fitreps.

*Wants to gain a competitive edge in "passing" all selection boards.

*Doesn't like to continually start writing Eval and Fitrep narratives from "scratch."

*Doesn't quite know how to word or document performance or potential.

*Wants to submit good, effective write-ups to impress the "boss."

This guide covers the "NUTS & BOLTS" of Fitreps and Evals--What should be in the narrative, how it should be worded, where the information should be placed, how it should be formatted, etc.

This guide contains:

*Instruction, direction, and guidance (with precisely worded samples) on how to submit smooth, finished Evals and Fitreps in the format and style that will positively influence selection boards.

*More than 600 ready-to-use phrases/bullets.

*Almost 500 of the most popular, descriptive adjectives.

*LDO/CWO Candidate information with 20+ Command endorsement samples.

*CPO, SCPO, & MCPO Selection Board Information (& worksheet samples)

*Brag Sheets...More...More

NAVY AND MARINE CORPS PERFORMANCE WRITING GUIDE

This 300+ Page Writing Guide picks up where the *ENLISTED EVAL AND OFFICER FITREP WRITING GUIDE* leaves off on Evals and Fitreps. PLUS, the following additional ALL NEW MATERIAL:

*Superior and Substandard Sections in every area of performance.

*Personal Awards (Navy Achievement/Commendation Medals, etc.).

*Sailor of the Month, Quarter, Year--Samples and Information.

*2,000 WORD DICTIONARY Alphabetical listing of the MOST USED ADJEC-TIVES, NOUNS, and VERBS in the English language on PERSONAL PERFOR-MANCE and PERSONALITY TRAITS...With definitions.

*2,000 WORD THESAURUS Grouped in unique, ready, and easy to use sections by SUPERIOR-TO-SUBSTANDARD PERFORMANCE, AND by PERFORMANCE and PERSONALITY TRAIT sections.

*2,500 BULLETS Ready to use. FAVORABLE AND UNFAVORABLE Sections.

More...More...More...

ORDER FORM

(Prices guaranteed through June 1991)

Military Purchase Orders Accepted.

Professional Management Spectrum, Inc.

P. O. Box 30330 • Pensacola, FL 32503 • Phone (904) 435-2584/2594

ORDERS ONLY: 1 (800) 346-6114   FAX: (904) 435-6923

TITLE	QTY	TOTAL
ENLISTED EVAL & OFFICER FITREP WRITING GUIDE (For Navy Use) ($21.95)		
NAVY & MARINE CORPS PERFORMANCE WRITING GUIDE ($23.95)		
THE DEFINITIVE PERFORMANCE WRITING GUIDE (For military & civilian use) ($25.95)		
FITNESS REPORT WRITING GUIDE FOR MARINES ($21.95)		
NAVY-WIDE EXAMINATION ADVANCEMENT GUIDE FOR E-3/4/5 ($21.95)		
NAVY-WIDE EXAMINATION ADVANCEMENT GUIDE FOR E-6/7 ($21.95)		
TAPE-SET - 600 QUESTIONS/ANSWERS FOR THE E-4/5 MILITARY LEADERSHIP EXAM (On 3 Audio Tapes) ($29.95)		
TAPE-SET - 600 QUESTIONS/ANSWERS FOR THE E-6/7 MILITARY LEADERSHIP EXAM (On 3 Audio Tapes) ($29.95)		
ENLISTED AVIATION WARFARE SPECIALIST (EAWS) STUDY GUIDE ($25.95)		
ENLISTED SURFACE WARFARE SPECIALIST (ESWS) STUDY GUIDE (Avail Summer '90) ($25.95)		
WRITING GUIDE FOR ARMY EFFICIENCY REPORTS ($23.95)		
WRITING GUIDE FOR AIR FORCE EFFICIENCY REPORTS ($23.95)		
SHIPPING: Add $1.50 (Regular Mail) OR: Add $3.00 (Air Mail) **(Per Book/Tape)**		
Florida Addresses Add **6%** Sales Tax		
100% REFUND GUARANTEE: If not competely satisfied with any book(s), return within 30 days and receive 100% refund. **Immediate Shipment.** All books shipped within 3 days-no delays. All books shipped Fourth Class Mail unless Air Mail specified.	**TOTAL**	**$**

Signature (Credit Card Orders Only)

METHOD OF PAYMENT: ☐ Check ☐ Money Order ☐ VISA ☐ MasterCard ☐ AMEX

Card No.

Expiration Date:

MAIL ORDER TO:

RANK/NAME_____

ADDRESS_____

THE DEFINITIVE PERFORMANCE WRITING GUIDE

This **475+ page book** is packed full of information that allows you to become your own successful wordsmith.

With this book you can write **military**, **government**, or **civilian** performance appraisals.

This book contains:

*5,500+ **bullet phrase** statements

*2,300+ **words** grouped in convenient, highly descriptive **"word banks."**

*2,200+ **words** in 2 unique **thesaurus chapters** on performance

This book give you simple, straight-forward, and **EASY-TO-USE** information for you to use when writing on **anyone's PERFORMANCE, BEHAVIOR, or CHARACTER.**

PERSONAL PERFORMANCE CHAPTERS ON:

1 - SUPERIOR PERFORMANCE

2 - ABOVE AVERAGE PERFORMANCE

3 - EFFECTIVE PERFORMANCE

4 - BELOW AVERAGE PERFORMANCE

5 - UNSATISFACTORY PERFORMANCE

Sections in each chapter provide:

  *A selective **"WORD BANK"**

  *A wide variety of ready-made **BULLET PHRASE statements**

  * A selection of phrases that allow you to add personal information to **complete the phrase statement**

OTHER CHAPTERS COVERING BOTH FAVORABLE AND UNFAVORABLE WRITING ON:

1 - PERSONALITY & WORK RELATIONSHIPS

2 - LEADERSHIP, SUPERVISION & MANAGEMENT

3 - SELF-EXPRESSION & COMMUNICATION SKILLS

OTHER UNIQUE CHAPTERS IN THIS BOOK COVER:

*A selection of **ACTIVE-ACTION words** to add **POWER** and **SKILL** to your particular writing style.

*Valuable information on exactly **how to construct writings**

*Important **DOs** and **DON'Ts**

***OBJECTIVE** and **SUBJECTIVE** analysis information

*A **PREPARATION CHECK-LIST**

*Helpful **writing hints**

***KEY WORDS** to assist you in evaluating **anyone's** performance level

*A **"BELL CURVE"** covering marking or ranking distribution

*MUCH, MUCH MORE...

SEE ORDER FORM TO OBTAIN YOUR COPY

ENLISTED AVIATION **WARFARE SPECIALIST** **(EAWS) STUDY GUIDE**	**ENLISTED SURFACE** **WARFARE SPECIALIST** **(ESWS) STUDY GUIDE** (Due out Summer 1990)

The *Enlisted Aviation Warfare Specialist (EAWS) Study Guide*:

*300+PAGES

*1,000+ DETAILED and IN-DEPTH ANSWERS to all EAWS PQS questions, covered in 23 chapters.

*OVER 85 PICTURES/ILLUSTRATIONS to reinforce information and enhance retention of subject matter.

*More...More...More

The *Enlisted Surface Warfare Specialist (ESWS) Study Guide*:

*COMPLETE, IN-DEPTH DISCUSSION AND ANSWERS for all ESWS PQS questions.

*GREATLY REDUCES THE TIME REQUIRED for COMPLETE PREPARATION for ESWS qualification board.

*SPECIAL DAMAGE CONTROL, FIREFIGHTING, and CBR DEFENSE Sections with hundreds of questions/answers often asked by qualification boards.

Primary uses of these Study Guides:

* Studying for the EAWS & ESWS Qualification Board.

* Ready reference for COs, XOs, Command Master Chiefs, and others.

These Study Guides:

* Can be used by anyone who wants the competitive edge in PASSING the EAWS & ESWS Qualification Board.

* Were constructed for the individual who wants the COMPLETE, CORRECT answers to the questions asked.

ORDER FORM

(Prices guaranteed through June 1991)

Military Purchase Orders Accepted.

Professional Management Spectrum, Inc.

P. O. Box 30330 • Pensacola, FL 32503 • Phone (904) 435-2584/2594

ORDERS ONLY: 1 (800) 346-6114   FAX: (904) 435-6923

TITLE	QTY	TOTAL
ENLISTED EVAL & OFFICER FITREP WRITING GUIDE (For Navy Use) ($21.95)		
NAVY & MARINE CORPS PERFORMANCE WRITING GUIDE ($23.95)		
THE DEFINITIVE PERFORMANCE WRITING GUIDE (For military & civilian use) ($25.95)		
FITNESS REPORT WRITING GUIDE FOR MARINES ($21.95)		
NAVY-WIDE EXAMINATION ADVANCEMENT GUIDE FOR E-3/4/5 ($21.95)		
NAVY-WIDE EXAMINATION ADVANCEMENT GUIDE FOR E-6/7 ($21.95)		
TAPE-SET - 600 QUESTIONS/ANSWERS FOR THE E-4/5 MILITARY LEADERSHIP EXAM (On 3 Audio Tapes) ($29.95)		
TAPE-SET - 600 QUESTIONS/ANSWERS FOR THE E-6/7 MILITARY LEADERSHIP EXAM (On 3 Audio Tapes) ($29.95)		
ENLISTED AVIATION WARFARE SPECIALIST (EAWS) STUDY GUIDE ($25.95)		
ENLISTED SURFACE WARFARE SPECIALIST (ESWS) STUDY GUIDE (Avail Summer '90) ($25.95)		
WRITING GUIDE FOR ARMY EFFICIENCY REPORTS ($23.95)		
WRITING GUIDE FOR AIR FORCE EFFICIENCY REPORTS ($23.95)		
SHIPPING: Add $1.50 (Regular Mail) **OR**: Add $3.00 (Air Mail) **(Per Book/Tape)**		
Florida Addresses Add **6%** Sales Tax		
100% REFUND GUARANTEE: If not competely satisfied with any book(s), return within 30 days and receive 100% refund. **TOTAL**	**$**	
Immediate Shipment. All books shipped within 3 days-no delays. All books shipped Fourth Class Mail unless Air Mail specified.		

Signature (Credit Card Orders Only)
_____

METHOD OF PAYMENT: ☐ Check ☐ Money Order ☐ VISA ☐ MasterCard ☐ AMEX

Card No.

Expiration Date:

MAIL ORDER TO:

RANK/NAME_____

ADDRESS_____

_____

NAVY-WIDE EXAMINATION ADVANCEMENT GUIDE FOR E-3/4/5
&
NAVY-WIDE EXAMINATION ADVANCEMENT GUIDE FOR E-6/E-7

THE AUTHOR

The recently-retired author is **uniquely qualified** to write on the subject of Navy enlisted advancement. **Credentials include:**

*Advanced from E-1 to E-9 in 18 years.

*Navy-wide Exam writer for 4 years

*Author of 2 Navy Rate Training Manuals & Correspondence Courses.

*Graduate of Examination & Rate Training Manual Development School.

*6 Years Navy Instructor Experience.

*Presented lectures and briefs on how to prepare for and pass Navy-wide exams at major Naval installations.

*During distinguished Navy career, not a single subordinate EVER failed a Navy-wide exam.

THE BOOKS

Each book has almost **300 pages,** including:

**100+pages of essential exam preparation and performance information on:

EASY-TO-LEARN procedures, principles, and steps on HOW TO **GET THE EDGE ON THE TEST AND THE COMPETITION.

**PREPARATION PROCEDURES for Navy-Wide exams.

**INFORMATIVE INSIGHT on how Navy Writers develop exams.

**ESSENTIAL "RULES" TO FOLLOW for exam taking and preparation

**EXAM STRATEGY. How to INCREASE YOUR "GUESS FACTOR" and get the correct answers without knowing the answer.

**EASY MEMORY AND STUDY HABIT improvement methods.

**CAREER AND EDUCATION OPPORTUNITIES reference section.

**BONUS:

**600 QUESTIONS AND ANSWERS on the Navy-Wide LEADERSHIP EXAMS.

The E-6/7 BOOK has a **special section on **CPO & OFFICER SELECTION BOARDS.** An inside look with inside information that every serious-minded advancement candidate should know.

NOW AVAILABLE ON CASSETTE TAPE

**600 Questions and Answers for Leadership Exams. Two tape sets available. One tape set contains 600 Question/Answers for E-4 & E-5 Military Leadership Exam. Other tape set contains 600 Questions/Answers for E-6 & E-7 Leadership Exam. See Order Form.

Books Published By
Professional Management Spectrum, Inc.

Enlisted Eval and Officer Fitrep Writing Guide (For Navy Use)

The Definitive Performance Writing Guide
(For military, government, or civilian appraisals)

Navy & Marine Corps Performance Writing Guide

Fitness Report Writing Guide for Marines

Writing Guide for Air Force Efficiency Reports

Writing Guide for Army Efficiency Reports

Navy-Wide Examination Advancement Guide for E-3/4/5

Navy-Wide Examination Advancement Guide for E-6/7

TAPE SET "600 Military Leadership Questions/Answers for E-4/5"

TAPE SET "600 Military Leadership Questions/Answers for E-6/7"

Enlisted Aviation Warfare Specialist (EAWS) Study Guide

Enlisted Surface Warfare Specialist (ESWS) Study Guide

PROFESSIONAL MANAGEMENT SPECTRUM, INC.
P.O. BOX 30330
PENSACOLA, FL 32503
PHONE (904) 435-2584/2594

ENLISTED EVAL AND OFFICER FITREP
WRITING GUIDE

First Edition Copyright © 1984

Second Edition Copyright © 1989

Updated 1990

by Douglas L. Drewry
All rights reserved

For information address:

PROFESSIONAL MANAGEMENT SPECTRUM, INC.
P.O. BOX 30330
PENSACOLA, FL 32503

ISBN: 0-9623673-1-1

PRINTED IN THE UNITED STATES OF AMERICA

TABLE OF CONTENTS

FORWARD

Almost all of the material in this guide is equally applicable when writing on officer or enlisted personnel.

The printed material in one chapter can be used with the subject matter of another chapter. Two chapters (the "Bullets" and "Word Picture Personality" chapters) were constructed specifically to have universal application on any subject matter in this guide.

The sample write-ups provided in this guide reflect several writing styles. They give the reader a variety of ideas on how subject material can be written. When drafting performance appraisals, remember you are writing to "sell" the evaluee to selection boards by covering that individual's performance, ability, and potential. All writing styles in this guide accomplish this objective.

There is enough material available in this guide to form a sound base in the construction of hundreds of individual write-ups, each with its own uniqueness and individuality.

CHAPTER

ONE

EVAL

&

FITREP

WRITING

GUIDANCE

CHAPTER 1

EVAL & FITREP WRITING GUIDANCE   PAGE

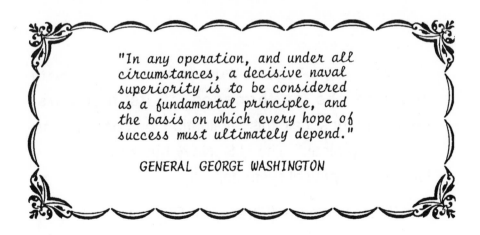

"In any operation, and under all circumstances, a decisive naval superiority is to be considered as a fundamental principle, and the basis on which every hope of success must ultimately depend."

GENERAL GEORGE WASHINGTON

PERFORMANCE APPRAISAL

INTRODUCTION AND INFORMATION

Where you stand on an issue often depends on where you sit.

Every large organization has some means to evaluate the performance of its members. Administrator's call this evaluation process "performance appraisal." The U.S. Navy has two basic performance appraisal systems:

-Fitness Reports (Fitreps) for Officers

-Enlisted Evaluations for Enlisted

In this guide the term "performance appraisal" applies equally to the Fitrep and the enlisted evaluation.

PRIMARY OBJECTIVES OF GIVING PERFORMANCE APPRAISALS

1. Identify advancement, retention and future duty potential.

2. Provide feedback to the evaluee.

PERFORMANCE MEASURED.

1. PERSONAL TRAITS - How something is done (for example, the leadership, initiative, etc. used or applied to accomplish something).

2. JOB PERFORMANCE - What and how much is done.

3. JOB BEHAVIOR - Appearance, adaptability, behavior, etc.

OBJECTIVE AND SUBJECTIVE ANALYSIS.

OBJECTIVE ANALYSIS should be used whenever possible to document an individual's performance. Objective analysis means to quantify performance results. How much was done? What was done? Use hours, time, percent, dollars, etc.

SUBJECTIVE ANALYSIS is the evaluator's perceptions, beliefs, or thoughts on how something was accomplished. This is an analysis of a person's "inner" qualities (or personality) and must be based on observations over a period of time. Subjective analysis is used to describe what prompted or caused an individual to do something (personal traits such as leadership, imagination, etc.).

PERFORMANCE APPRAISAL

PREPARATION CHECK-LIST

The more knowledge and tools an evaluator has at his disposal the better. The following information should be reviewed **PRIOR TO** committing a subordinate's performance to print.

1. All performance appraisals should be handled discreetly. They should be worked on in private.

2. Rough copies of past performance appraisals should be retained on file for reference in the next reporting period.

3. Insofar as practicable, reporting seniors should grade all performance appraisals of the same competitive category at one time. This will facilitate comparative grading.

4. Endeavor to obtain a just and equitable spread in the marks assigned to a comparative group.

5. Do not gravitate toward either a gratuitously high or rigidly severe policy of grading. The Navy is plagued by general over-assessment of average performers and occasional under assessment of "top performers."

This serves to reduce the promotional opportunities of the "best qualified."

6. Exercise care to mark objectively, avoiding any tendency which might allow general impressions, a single incident or a particular trait, characteristic, or quality to influence other marks unduly.

7. When uncertain, due to limited observation, as to the appropriate evaluation of any rating area, mark the "Not Observed" block rather than assign a "middle-of-the-road" mark.

8. Avoid marking a new person somewhat lower than he/she deserves in order to reflect improved performance in subsequent performance appraisals. This malpractice can result in unjust advancement or assignment actions.

9. Before beginning to write, check over available performance data and determine which category you are going to place an individual being reported on:

   a. Head and shoulders above his contemporaries --promote now.

   b. Above many contemporaries--promote above most.

c. Good performer--promote with majority of contemporaries.

d. Behind peer group performance--do not promote.

When a decision has been reached, write a performance appraisal that will support and justify your position.

10. The "head and shoulders" performers should be immediately identified at the start of the narrative. The remaining write-up must justify and reinforce your position.

11. Ensure that realistic marks are assigned individuals whose performance of duty has been manifestly unsatisfactory. Impersonal grading and concise statements of fact best serve overall interests under such circumstances.

12. Conversely, ensure that due recognition is accorded when an individual demonstrates truly outstanding or exceptional professional competence and potential. In such cases accentuate the positive. State major accomplishments that have been achieved. More importantly, comment constructively on capacity

or potential for future increased responsibility or promotion.

13. If the command has made an outstanding performance during the reporting period, an individual's contribution to this effect should be included. Of course, the converse is true.

14. After completion of a performance appraisal, review previous worksheets on the same person, if available, to ensure that any changes in the marks on the current appraisal are intended. Any significant shift of marks in reports signed by the same reporting senior must be substantiated by the narrative.

15. When making subsequent reports on the same person, guard against repetitive phraseology, as this will reflect lack of thought.

16. Before submitting a smooth performance appraisal, analyze the narrative to make sure that what is meant to be said is, in fact, actually being said, giving careful thought not only to what chosen words mean to the evaluator, but also how they may be construed by a selection board.

17. When the performance appraisal is finished, review it to ensure that:

a. All parts are consistent (marks & narrative agree).

b. The trend in performance (increase or decrease) is correctly conveyed.

18. Bear in mind that performance appraisal narratives reflect the degree and extent in which evaluators measure up to their moral obligation. And, an evaluator's write-up may be used to judge his/her performance.

19. Words are both valuable and dangerous tools. Choose them carefully.

20. Words mean what they say. Review the following:

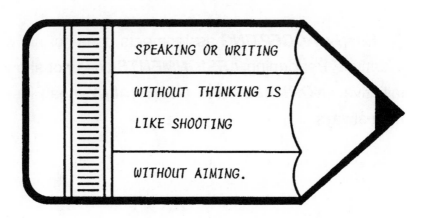

SPEAKING OR WRITING WITHOUT THINKING IS LIKE SHOOTING WITHOUT AIMING.

POTENTIAL   CAPACITY   ABILITY

To indicate that an individual has these qualities without supporting evidence will register to a selection board as "insufficient data."   A person can have **POTENTIAL**, **CAPACITY**, or **ABILITY** and yet accomplish nothing.   Write how these qualities were demonstrated.

TRIES   STRIVES

Someone can **TRY** or **STRIVE** without accomplishing anything. As above, note how these qualities were positively demonstrated.

ACCEPTS ASSIGNED NORMALLY GENERALLY

Simply **ACCEPTING** assignments does not show initiative. Performing **ASSIGNMENTS** does not show initiative. **NORMALLY** and **GENERALLY** mean less than always.

AVERAGE   ABOVE AVERAGE   EXCELLENT
OUTSTANDING

These words have "canned" meanings and understandings in the Navy. *ABOVE AVERAGE* is generally assumed to mean less than *EXCELLENT* or *OUTSTANDING*. *AVERAGE* means less than *ABOVE AVERAGE*, etc.. If you are going to place someone's performance in one of these categories, be sure to choose the correct word(s).

DO CHECK LIST:

-DO submit performance appraisals on time and in correct format.

-DO write performance appraisals directed TO selection boards.

-DO write on how someone contributed above or below what is normally expected.

-DO write to express, not impress.

-DO be fair, honest, and objective.

-DO comment on growth potential and qualifications for advancement and future duty assignments.

-DO write on hard, pertinent facts, not "faint praises" without substance.

-DO use short, concise "bullets" or complete sentences with proper grammar.

-DO use underline to highlight key areas only.

-DO include specific extracurricular activities.

DON'T CHECK LIST:

-DON'T assign marks that are inconsistent with the narrative.

-DON'T write performance appraisals directed TO the individual.

-DON'T assign exceptionally high/low marks without comments in the narrative that clearly distinguish the performance.

-DON'T include minor, isolated, or insignificant imperfections which do not affect performance. Someone can be "Four-O" without being perfect.

-DON'T use glittering generalities which go on and on without saying anything useful.

-DON'T use long words when shorter words will do.

-DON'T be verbose or redundant.

-DON'T restate the job description in the narrative. That space is too valuable.

-DON'T write "During the period of this report" or words to that effect. It is understood, unless otherwise stated, that all actions and events in a performance appraisal occurred during the reporting period being covered. Again, narrative space is too valuable.

-DON'T start too many sentences with the same: Chief... He... He... His... Chief... His... etc.. Reading becomes sluggish and boring and shows lack of attention or ability on the part of the drafter.

-DON'T use a person's name without associated rank. For example, do not write "Jones is..."; instead, it should be "LT/Chief/Seaman Jones is..." A performance appraisal is an official document and an individual's rank should always accompany his/her name.

-DON'T use the term "ratee." It is too impersonal and impresses no one.

"You may fire when you are ready, Gridley."

COMMODORE GEORGE DEWEY

PERFORMANCE APPRAISAL

DRAFTING THE NARRATIVE

1. <u>OBJECTIVE</u>. Performance appraisals should be drafted with two objectives in mind. These objectives are:

a. To document, in SPECIFIC terms, <u>what</u> an individual contributed to Navy, command, and department/division mission effectiveness and accomplishment; and,

b. To document the <u>subjective</u> "inner" qualities demonstrated by an individual on <u>how</u> performance was accomplished.

2. <u>GUIDANCE</u>.

a. <u>BE POSITIVE</u>: Any shortcoming or deficiency mentioned in the narrative should be significant, either in terms of performance or potential. At any level in an organization some occasional, routine guidance is necessary. If the comment is made that someone requires occasional instruction or guidance, that means he/she requires more instruction or guidance than would normally be expected. In effect, comments on minor deficiencies are automatically magnified when they are included in the narrative.

b. <u>BE CONCISE</u>: A direct hard-hitting write-up is better than an elegant one--concentrate more on content and specific accomplishments.

c. <u>BE FACTUAL</u>: Quantify individual achievements and accomplishments when possible.

d. <u>BE SPECIFIC</u>: A few well worded phrases or sentences on individual accomplishment and achievement mean much more than pages on billet description, command employment, etc...

e. <u>BE OBJECTIVE</u>: To the maximum extent possible, comment on quantifiable "objective" accomplishments, not on "subjective" personal notions.

3. <u>STRUCTURE</u>. The following performance appraisal structure has won wide acceptance in the Navy and is highly favored by Navy selection boards. Format in order given.

    a. OPENING FORMAT.

    b. JOB ACCOMPLISHMENT.

    c. PERSONAL AND BEHAVIORAL TRAITS.

    d. CLOSING FORMAT.

The following pages deal more specifically with this structure format.

PERFORMANCE APPRAISAL

OPENING FORMAT

The most closely read sentences in a performance appraisal are the opening sentences. The opening should be a powerful and persuasive statement--an "attention getter" to immediately capture the attention of the reader. The opening format should be limited to three themes:

1. Overview of best attributes/performance (or the converse for substandard performers);

2. Potential (for top performers); and,

3. Awards or other forms of recognition received.

The opening format sets the "theme" for the remaining narrative.

SAMPLE OPENING FORMAT

...(name) is an exceptionally well qualified (peer group). Extremely well organized, mission-oriented and empathic with his subordinates and the work environment. He has infused the (organization) with his enthusiasm and dedication. Unlimited potential. Awarded Navy Achievement Medal for ...

...(name) professional talents, dedication, and aggressive work habits are an asset to the (organization). Virtually unlimited potential. Awarded Letter of Commendation for ...

...(name) is an outstanding manager and organizer who is willing to accept any assignment regardless of scope. Boundless potential. Selected as ... of the Year.

...(name) is an energetic, industrious, and conscientious individual who has proven himself time after time to be a top performer. (Potential...Awards)

...(name) has continually proven himself to be a (peer group) of exemplary character and outstanding ability. (Potential...Awards)

...(name) professional knowledge, self-motivation, and determined, tireless efforts have made excellent contributions to the efficient functioning of (organization). (Potential ...Awards)

...(name) possesses the character, initiative, and resourcefulness to accept and accomplish the most demanding tasks. A proven leader of unbounded potential. (Awards)

...(name) is an extremely intelligent and dynamic leader who thrives on challenge. (Potential...Awards)

...(name) performance has been of the highest caliber. His self-confidence and acute awareness of what is going on around him have lead to measurable improvement in the operation of (organization). (Potential...Awards)

...(name) is an energetic and methodical organizer, leader, and manager who carries out all assignments in an exceptionally competent manner. (Potential...Awards)

...(name) is an exceptional example of a leader and manager. (Potential...Awards)

...(name) excels wherever he is assigned. He has been an invaluable manager, counselor, and source of technical knowledge in every area of responsibility. (Potential...Awards)

...(name) is a superb manager and organizer whose demonstrated expertise as a leader has measurably improved improved the operational effectiveness of (organization). (Potential...Awards)

...(name) is meticulously accurate with a great sense of responsibility for the quality of his work. (Potential...Awards)

...(name) is a proven professional in every sense. His courage of conviction and strong moral character fosters high morale, esprit de corps, and a total winning attitude. (Potential ... Awards)

...(name) performance is underscored by pride, self-improvement, and accomplishment. (Potential...Awards)

...(name) is extremely conscientious, a professional whose managerial abilities and administrative skills are unequalled. (Potential...Awards)

...(name) performance, both professionally and militarily, is nothing short of outstanding. A top performer. (Potential...Awards)

...(name) is an excellent (peer group) who consistently demonstrates superlative performance. His ability to accomplish all assignments, assigned or assumed, in superior fashion have made him a valuable asset to the (organization). (Potential...Awards)

...(name) is not only a skilled (job), he is also a dedicated leader whose standards of integrity and military bearing are of the highest quality. (Potential...Awards)

...(name) has demonstrated outstanding professional qualities, sound, mature judgement, and an exemplary mannerism in his duties as (job/billet). (Potential...Awards)

...(name) sustained superior performance has been an inspiration to each member of (organization). The deep respect he enjoys from all hands manifests his superlative qualities of leadership, integrity, and professional knowledge. (Potential ...Awards)

...Intelligent, industrious, and articulate, (name) is aggressive and meticulous in completion of all duties. (Potential...Awards)

...(name) performance regularly exceeds job requirements. He is unusually accurate, thorough, and effective. (Potential...Awards)

...(name) duties as (job) have been skillfully performed. (Potential...Awards)

...Motivated, concerned, and involved. (name) is especially effective in leadership of people and management of material. (Potential... Awards)

...Exceptionally talented. Personable, innovative, and industrious. (name) is a top performer who consistently produces outstanding results. (Potential...Awards)

...(name) is alert, quick, and responsive. Possessed with unusual perceptive common sense and a grasp of reality. (Potential...Awards)

...(name) is dependable and conscientious, using logic and foresight to develop priorities that are always consistent with command policy. (Potential...Awards)

...(name) is articulate and thorough. Attacks each job with zeal and enthusiasm, not content until every detail has been attended to and successfully completed. (Potential...Awards)

PERFORMANCE APPRAISAL

JOB ACCOMPLISHMENT

The **JOB ACCOMPLISHMENT** portion of a performance appraisal is used to document individual accomplishment and achievement in primary and collateral duties in relation to mission effectiveness.

For a good, hard-hitting write-up this section of the performance appraisal should cover two major items:

1. OBJECTIVE, specific job accomplishments; and,

2. SUBJECTIVE "inner" qualities or characteristics.

OBJECTIVE JOB ACCOMPLISHMENT.

Answer the questions:

-What was accomplished?

-Was accomplishment superior or inferior to the norm?

EXAMPLES:

-Qualified as OOD Inport in 2 months, less than half the normal time.

-Completed 6 correspondence courses.

-Researched, drafted, and implemented 10 SOPs and a division organization manual in first 2 months on the job, giving a total of 100 off-duty hours to these projects.

-Led 10-man watch team that earned an overall grade of 97% during REFTRA. Highest score among the 5 watch teams in the department.

-Received "OUTSTANDING" at 3 command personnel inspections.

"Inner" characteristics relate **HOW** or **WHAT POS-SESSED** a person to accomplish something. These "inner" qualities help to project a person's **POTEN-TIAL, WORTH**, and **VALUE** to the Navy. The chapter entitled "Word Picture Personality" has a comprehensive listing of appropriate words.

EXAMPLES: Imagination, initiative, tact, organized, etc...

Specific examples of how to combine the objective job accomplishment and the subjective "inner" characteristics can be found throughout the "Performance Appraisal Sample" chapter of this guide.

"The pen

is

mightier

than

the sword."

SHAKESPEARE

PERFORMANCE APPRAISAL

PERSONAL AND BEHAVIORAL TRAITS

This section of the performance appraisal narrative includes anything worthy of comment or necessary which has not been included in other sections. Items that would be appropriate in this section include:

1. ADAPTABILITY

2. APPEARANCE

3. BEHAVIOR

4. EDUCATION

5. COMMUNITY INVOLVEMENT

As in the Job Accomplishment section, objective and quantifiable performance should be coupled with subjective "inner" quality characteristic traits.

SAMPLE PERSONAL AND BEHAVIORAL TRAITS

...Smart, neat, dignified appearance.

...Fit and trim in posture, takes great pride in maintaining high standards of personal appearance and demeanor.

...Completed six correspondence courses not required of rate.

...Completed three off-duty college courses in pursuit of a Bachelor's Degree.

...Involved in extra curricular activities: President of ...; Spokesperson for ...; and, volunteers weekends to assist underprivileged ...

...A morale booster. Spreads sense of esprit de corps and good will throughout the command.

...Flawless military appearance and demeanor.

...Concerned and involved, imparts pride, motivation, and a sense of belonging.

...Possesses cooperative and friendly spirit, and a positive "can do" attitude.

...Has a good sense of humor, a polished manner, and radiates a sense of team spirit and cooperation.

...Demeanor promotes efficiency, trust, and high state of morale.

PERFORMANCE APPRAISAL

CLOSING FORMAT

The CLOSING FORMAT is another good place for a drafter to "sell" an individual to a selection board. Three subject areas should be covered in this section:

1. GROWTH POTENTIAL;

2. FUTURE DUTY RECOMMENDATION, and,

3. RECOMMENDATION FOR ADVANCEMENT.

GROWTH POTENTIAL (best wording includes)

...Virtually unlimited potential.

...Limitless potential.

...Unbounded potential.

...Extraordinary growth potential.

Hit YouR TARGEt

FUTURE DUTY RECOMMENDATION

ENLISTED

These examples can be used in conjunction with recommendations for instructor duty, recruiter duty, etc... In effect, these examples further show an individual's potential.

...Recommended to serve as a Command (Senior/Master) Chief aboard a major combatant or large shore command.

...Recommended for a Force Master Chief Billet.

...Recommended for duty as MCPO of the Navy.

(NOTE: If an individual is not an E-9, or competing for E-9, the above examples could be used stating that the individual is recommended for "future" duty in one of those jobs/billets.)

...Should be selectively detailed to only the most demanding and challenging billets, both ashore and afloat.

OFFICER

Recommendations for future duty for officers vary widely because of different career fields. Timing on when to fill this or that billet is important. In general, top performers should try to get recommended for <u>billets one or two pay grades above billet currently being filled.</u>

General guidance:

JUNIOR OFFICERS - Recommendation for Head of Department billet or Department Head School. Instructor duty (i.e. SWO School).

JUNIOR OFFICERS (LDO) - Officer in Charge, Head of Department, or XO duty as appropriate.

GENERAL - Advanced schooling such as postgraduate study.

- A good Fitrep signed by an operational admiral is always an asset. Consider staff duty.

FUTURE DUTY RECOMMENDATION CRITERIA

RECRUIT COMPANY COMMANDER

The recruit company commander is usually the new recruit's first encounter with a regular Navy person in a naval environment. The first impression imposed by the recruit company commander is most important. With this in mind, recommendations for this special assignment should be given to members who are authoritative leaders and who command the respect of their peers. They must be truly professional military persons. Personal appearance, military bearing, and pride in the Navy must be present in abundance.

"We have met the enemy and they are ours."

OLIVER HAZARD PERRY

JOINT/COMBINED STAFF, ATTACHE &

NAVAL HEADQUARTERS

These are special assignments that require a great amount of administrative ability. By administrative ability is meant the capacity to cope with excessive amounts of paperwork, disseminate data, and incorporate new policies as well as changes to existing policies. Also, along with his administrative abilities, he must be a good talker as well as a good listener. Of course, a high degree of professionalism, a great amount of military bearing and immaculate personal appearance cannot be overlooked.

INSTRUCTOR

An instructor is a learned person who conveys his knowledge to learners. In order to accomplish this, an instructor must be an outstanding communicator who is able to express himself fully and convey ideas in a clear and demonstrative manner. He must be able to attain the respect of his students through a combination of his subject knowledge, his military bearing, his personal appearance, and his other outward personal traits.

INDEPENDENT DUTY

The term "independent duty" is self-explanatory. Candidates for independent duty must be conscientious, industrious, reliable, resourceful, good decision-makers, have good insight, and possess high moral character.

Recommendations for special assignment should be made independent of an individual's stated preference. Evaluators should make their recommendations solely on their evaluation of an individual's potential for serving in that specific assignment.

MAAG/MISSION

MAAG members administer United States Military assistance planning and programming to military members of host foreign countries. Considerations to be taken into account when making recommendations for this type of assignment are appearance and military bearing, an ability to work directly with troops of a foreign nation, the member's ability to speak a foreign language (bilingual).

RECRUITER

A recruiter is a salesman for the Navy--he "sells" the Navy to young men and women. Therefore, a recruiter should first be an outstanding salesman. He should be a good talker and be able to interact with young people. He must have a clear understanding of the Naval structure and its policies and programs. Motivation, good physical shape, and pride in wearing his uniform are prerequisites for this type of assignment.

CAREER COUNSELOR

A career counselor is also a salesman. He not only sells a Navy career to reenlistees, but he sells the Navy's many opportunity programs to members at every level in the enlisted structure. He must be a good communicator and learned in all of the Navy's old and new policies, programs, and procedures. An interest in people and an understanding of their problems is necessary. Honesty, military bearing, and good personal appearance should also be included in considering a member for career counselor duty.

RECOMMENDATION FOR PROMOTION/ADVANCEMENT

ENLISTED

...Recommended for advancement.

...Highly recommended for advancement.

...Strongly recommended for advancement.

...Most strongly recommended for immediate advancement.

...I most strongly recommend (name) for immediate advancement to ... (signed by C.O.) Any time the word "I" is used and the performance appraisal is signed by the commanding officer, additional emphasis is added to the recommendation.

The below type of sentence would be appropriate for a top performer, whether or not that individual is currently eligible or intends to participate in an enlisted-to-officer program. The statement shows worth, value, and potential for greatly increased positions of trust and responsibility.

"I highly recommend (name) for a commission as a (CWO/LDO); he would be a welcomed addition to my wardroom."

Additional officer recommendation wording is located in the "CWO-LDO Endorsement" Section of this guide.

OFFICER

...Recommended for promotion with contemporaries.

...Recommended for promotion ahead of contemporaries.

...Highly recommended for accelerated/early promotion.

...(name) has earned my strongest recommendation for promotion ahead of contemporaries.

POTENTIAL, FUTURE DUTY, & ADVANCEMENT STATEMENT - ENLISTED

"(name) has <u>extraordinary growth potential</u>. He is <u>most strongly recommended for immediate advancement</u> to (peer group). Without reservation, <u>I recommend him for commission as a Limited Duty Officer</u>. He would be a welcomed addition to any wardroom. (name) should be <u>selectively detailed</u> to only the <u>most demanding and challenging billets</u>."

POTENTIAL, FUTURE DUTY, & PROMOTION STATEMENT - OFFICER

"(name) has <u>extraordinary growth potential</u>. <u>Most strongly recommended for accelerated promotion.</u> Recommended for <u>Department Head School</u> and follow-up assignment as Department Head aboard major combatant. <u>Detail selectively to most demanding billets</u>.

As noted elsewhere in this guide, <u>underline high points</u> in the narrative for emphasis.

PERFORMANCE APPRAISAL

GENERAL MARKING GUIDANCE

The qualities listed on the following tables represent broad guidelines. Other qualities should be judged for specific levels of performance by the reporting officer. Descriptions categorized as FIRST RATE are meant to build on or incorporate the descriptions listed as ABOVE EXPECTATIONS or SATISFACTORY. UNSATISFACTORY performance includes qualities listed in the BELOW EXPECTATIONS category as well as those in the UNSATISFACTORY category, and includes omissions of capabilities listed in SATISFACTORY, ABOVE EXPECTATIONS, and FIRST RATE categories.

PROFESSIONAL FACTORS

MILITARY KNOWLEDGE/PERFORMANCE

FIRST RATE
(4.0/3.8)
Works well independently; applies technical skills to job effectively; contributes extensively to command mission; has thorough understanding of complexities of job; analyses problems and readily implements best solution.

ABOVE EXPECTATIONS
(3.6/3.4)
Contributes to command objectives; accepts delegated authority; proposes solutions to difficult problems; sets and pursues goals in organized manner; asks questions when in doubt.

SATISFACTORY
(3.2/3.0)
Completes assigned tasks in a timely manner; requires limited supervision; evaluates information and applies problem solving; has good understanding of major duties; informs subordinates of changes.

BELOW EXPECTATIONS
(2.8/2.6)
Cannot complete duties completely or on time; requires routine supervision; cannot relate technical knowledge to work.

UNSATISFACTORY
(2.0/1.0)
Fails to fulfill requirements of job; requires constant assistance; misinterprets problems repeatedly.

PROFESSIONAL FACTORS

RATING KNOWLEDGE/PEFORMANCE

**FIRST RATE
(4.0/3.8)**

Works well independently; applies technical skills to job effectively; contributes extensively to command mission; has thorough understanding of complexities of job; analyses problem and readily implements best solution.

**ABOVE EXPECTATIONS
(3.6/3.4)**

Contributes to command objectives; accepts delegated authority; proposes solutions to difficult problems; sets and pursues goals in organized manner; asks questions when in doubt.

**SATISFACTORY
(3.2/3.0)**

Completes assigned tasks in a timely manner; requires limited supervision; evaluates information and applies to problem solving; has good understanding of major duties; informs subordinates of changes.

**BELOW EXPECTATIONS
(2.8/2.6)**

Cannot complete duties completely or on time; requires routine supervision; cannot relate technical knowledge to work.

**UNSATISFACTORY
(2.0/1.0)**

Fails to fulfill requirements of job; requires constant assistance; misinterprets problems repeatedly.

PERSONAL TRAITS

INITIATIVE

FIRST RATE
(4.0/3.8)
Has well defined goals for self-improvement; makes effort to produce only highest quality work; determines and follows most efficient plan of action; does not require supervisor's approval.

ABOVE EXPECTATIONS
(3.6/3.4)
Seeks additional responsibility, exhibits drive for self-improvement in education; anticipates difficulty and works to circumvent; promotes team work.

SATISFACTORY
(3.2/3.0)
Assumes duties in absence of supervision; accepts opportunities to learn; suggests improvements to system occasionally.

BELOW EXPECTATIONS
(2.8/2.6)
Is satisfied with accomplishing work without concern for quality; avoids added responsibility; requires guidance of supervision.

UNSATISFACTORY
(2.0/1.0)
Has no desire to improve self; does not perform unless specifically directed.

PERSONAL TRAITS

MILITARY BEARING

FIRST RATE
(4.0/3.8)
Wears uniform with pride; is immaculate in military and civilian dress; has impressive bearing.

ABOVE EXPECTATIONS
(3.6/3.4)
Has good posture; is neat and clean; demonstrates high personal grooming standards.

SATISFACTORY
(3.2/3.0)
Presents acceptable appearance routinely; is physically fit; keeps uniforms repaired; meets percent body fat standards.

BELOW EXPECTATIONS
(2.8/2.6)
Wears uniforms improperly; is occasionally careless of appearance; has poor posture.

UNSATISFACTORY
(2.0/1.0)
Is sloppy, unkempt, or does not meet percent of body fat standards; slouches; is a discredit to the Naval Service.

SELF EXPRESSION

SPEAKING & WRITING ABILITY

**FIRST RATE
(4.0/3.8)**

Submits flawless written product; projects ideas in the most straightforward, comprehensive manner, keeps reference file of personal notes on important papers.

**ABOVE EXPECTATIONS
(3.6/3.4)**

Is able to translate thoughts into clear, understandable sentences; submits written work in a timely fashion.

**SATISFACTORY
(3.2/3.0)**

Is able to print and write legibly; is able to prepare realistic evaluation reports; shows awareness of importance of neat, accurate correspondence; gets point across.

**BELOW EXPECTATIONS
(2.8/2.6)**

Cannot get meaning across in concise organized means on paper.

**UNSATISFACTORY
(2.0/1.0)**

Unable to write legibly; shows poor use of English grammar and composition.

MANAGEMENT & LEADERSHIP

DIRECTING

FIRST RATE
(4.0/3.8)
Promotes subordinate involvement in planning to maximize output; inspires subordinates to self-improvement; inspires complete respect and confidence of subordinates; provides challenge.

ABOVE EXPECTATIONS
(3.6/3.4)
Solicits constructive criticism to improve performance; capably evaluates subordinate skills for work assignment; delegates authority for good use of personnel resources.

SATISFACTORY
(3.2/3.0)
Influences subordinates to work consistently and accurately; keeps personnel informed; maintains morale while enforcing regulations; usually delegates responsibility effectively.

BELOW EXPECTATIONS
(2.8/2.6)
Dictates activity of subordinates; fails to inform members of change or upcoming events; cannot maintain morale or get job done.

UNSATISFACTORY
(2.0/1.0)
Ignores suggestions of subordinates to improve performance; inhibits subordinate self-improvement; fails to delegate authority properly.

MANAGEMENT & LEADERSHIP

COUNSELING

**FIRST RATE
(4.0/3.8)**

Maintains excellent rapport with subordinates; is always willing to assist those in and out of unit; studies personal desires and needs of each member to recommend opportunities; helps members advance in Navy or transition to civilian life.

**ABOVE EXPECTATIONS
(3.6/3.4)**

Discusses performance and improvement with members on a regular basis; suggests methods for professional and educational growth; shows sincere concern for subordinates.

**SATISFACTORY
(3.2/3.0)**

Counsels members on positive and negative qualities as required; possesses good knowledge of what Navy has to offer; shows good human understanding.

**BELOW EXPECTATIONS
(2.8/2.6)**

Counsels subordinates only if severe difficulties arise; shows little concern for welfare of subordinates.

**UNSATISFACTORY
(2.0/1.0)**

Fails to discuss any matters with subordinates; avoids members.

PERFORMANCE APPRAISAL

BAD EXAMPLES

NOTE: The following BAD EXAMPLES were actually found by an E-8/9 selection board while screening candidates' performance appraisals.

-Academic average of 82.25. Stood 2 in a class of 1.

-The best Personnelman I have ever seen. He is a better PNC than I ever was. Select him for E-8 now. He's better qualified than I was and you picked me. (signed by CAPT)

-His military appearance remains uncompared within the command.

-Frequently reluctant to assume responsibility or exert authority. Highly recommended for warrant officer.

-While his dress is always neat and proper, his protruding stomach detracts from his overall excellent appearance.

-Consistently reluctant to assume a new job, but once the job is started...the reluctance is gone.

-Has a high degree of self confidence, but this should not be a stumbling block for long.

-Gets along extremely well with all classes of people from four star admirals to seaman and even the sanitorial help.

-An excellent example of equal opportunity in action, he treats everyone the same rotten way.

-Her ability to associate freely with both the rank and file has contributed significantly to the morale of the legal office.

-His transfer will be sorely missed by this command.

-There is NO position within the military structure, rate or rank, which is beyond this man's ability.

-He can do "anything better than anybody."

-With his personality, he would make friends with the Enemy.

-Has a tendency to impress officials and superiors with knowledge and expertise in areas where his knowledge is extremely inadequate.

CHAPTER TWO

START YOUR OWN

EVAL & FITREP

PROGRAM

CHAPTER 2

START YOUR OWN EVAL

& FITREP PROGRAM

As an added convenience, this information is presented in a format that will allow commands, departments, or divisions to incorporate this material into a local directive with minimum time and effort.

Permission is hereby granted by the Author for the material in this chapter (Chapter 2) to be reproduced for use on a local basis (i.e. individual divisions and departments). This permission does not extend to use in the civilian sector. Additionally, copyright protection makes it unlawful to reproduce any of the material in this book for resale in any form.

SECTION I

ADMINISTRATION AND PROCESSING OF ENLISTED EVALUATIONS

Subj: Administration & Processing of Enlisted Evaluations

Encl: (1) Evaluation Schedule

(2) Grading/Ranking Sheet

(3) Individual Input Sheet

1. <u>Purpose</u>. To provide policy guidance on the administration and processing of enlisted evaluations.

2. <u>Discussion</u>.

a. Enlisted evaluations are an important part of every service record and every possible effort will be made within (organization) to ensure that:

(1) Evaluations are processed in a timely fashion; and,

(2) Individuals are evaluated and ranked according to their value to the Navy and their contribution to command mission, goals, and objectives.

b. There are two tasks involved in performance evaluation:

(1) Relative grading and ranking within (organization); and,

(2) Detailed documentation of individual performance (the narrative write-up). The schedule at

enclosure (1) was developed to permit as much concurrency as possible in these two separate but related tasks. The initial effort is on developing an equitable grading and ranking (i.e. no narrative write-up). Once this is accomplished, work can begin on drafting the written narratives.

3. <u>Policy</u>. It is intended that each individual be able to review his/her evaluation on the closing date of the appropriate reporting period (for regular reports). The time-window due dates--as set forth in enclosure (1)--must be followed to ensure timely submission and to prevent processing bottlenecks. Evaluation narratives should not be accumulated and forwarded in groups; rather, each narrative should be forwarded for review as it is completed.

4. <u>Action</u>. The following specific actions are directed in the administration and processing of enlisted evaluations.

a. All evaluation write-up inputs will be typed and double-spaced. The narrative and job description sections will be submitted on separate sheets of paper.

b. Enlisted evaluations will be processed according to the schedule set forth in enclosure (1).

c. Department and division grading and ranking will be accomplished within the time frames of enclosure (1). Division grading and ranking will be recorded and forwarded on the appropriate form in enclosure (2). Final department grading and ranking will be recorded on the appropriate form in enclosure (2) and retained by the Head of Department.

d. Each evaluation narrative will be forwarded in a separate folder.

e. Each person being evaluated will be given the opportunity to provide an individual input to his/her evaluation using enclosure (3). (NOTE: Enclosure (3) is a variation of the standard Navy individual input sheet, and. allows for additional information input not included on the standard Navy form.)

EVALUATION SCHEDULE

ANNUAL EVALUATION SCHEDULE CYCLE

TIME WINDOW LATEST EARLIEST	EVENT/ACTIVITY
-8 weeks	Division Officer assemble key personnel, review material on file (IPRs, etc), and determine recommended marks and overall ranking.
-6 weeks -7 weeks	Division Officer: (1) Complete division marks/ranking and forward to deparment. (2) Assemble all information necessary to complete eval (job description, etc.). (3) Commence write-up drafts based on submitted marks/ranking.
-5 weeks -6weeks	Department/Command approve marks/ranking & provide feedback to division officers.
-4 weeks -5 weeks	Division officers forward completed evals to department.
-3 weeks -4 weeks	Head of Department review/approve evals (forward for higher review as necessary).
-2 weeks -3 weeks	Smooth type evals, proof read, and prepare for approving official's signature.
-1 week -2 weeks	Approving officer sign evaluations.
END OF REPORTING PERIOD	(1) Division officer (and others if required) review evaluations with individuals. (2) Individuals sign evals. (3) Division retain/destroy desired material and forward official evaluation copies.

Encl (1)

The recommended "TIME WINDOW" and the accompanying"- WEEKS" in the "EARLIEST" and "LATEST" columns should be converted to actual calendar dates.

EXAMPLE:

END OF REPORTING PERIOD	30 JUNE
-1 WEEK	23 JUNE
-2 WEEKS	16 JUNE
-3 WEEKS	9 JUNE
-4 WEEKS	1 JUNE
-5 WEEKS	23 MAY
-6 WEEKS	16 MAY
-7 WEEKS	9 MAY
-8 WEEKS	1 MAY

The "LATEST" and "EARLIEST" columns on the samples on the following pages are left blank so that the pages can be reproduced locally and filled-in with the appropriate dates.

Encl (1)

EVALUATION SCHEDULE

ANNUAL EVALUATION SCHEDULE CYCLE

TIME WINDOW LATEST EARLIEST	EVENT/ACTIVITY
....	Division Officer assemble key personnel, review material on file (IPRs, etc), and determine recommended marks and overall ranking.
....	Division Officer: (1) Complete division marks/ranking and forward to department. (2) Assemble all information necessary to complete eval (job description, etc.). (3) Commence write-up drafts based on submitted marks/ranking.
....	Department/Command approve marks/ranking & provide feedback to division officers.
....	Division officers forward completed evals to department.
....	Head of Department review/ approve evals (forward for higher review as necessary).
....	Smooth type evals, proof read, and prepare for approving official's signature.
....	Approving officer sign evaluations.
....	(1) Division officer (and others if required) review evaluations with individuals. (2) Individuals sign evals. (3) Division retain/destroy desired material and forward official evaluation copies.

Encl (1)

EVALUATION SCHEDULE

TRANSFER (& OTHER) EVALUATION SCHEDULE

TIME WINDOW

LATEST	EARLIEST	EVENT/ACTIVITY
-30 days		Division officer ensure personnel working on evaluation input.
-17 days	-24 days	Division officer review/approve eval (forward for review as necessary)
-10 days	-17 days	Smooth type eval, proof read, and prepare for approving official's signature
-3 days	-10 days	Approving officer sign evaluation
-1 day	-3 days	(1) Division officer review evaluation with individual. (2) Individual sign evaluation. (3) Division officer retain/destroy desired material and forward official evaluation copies.

Encl (1)

EVALUATION SCHEDULE

TRANSFER (& OTHER) EVALUATION SCHEDULE

TIME WINDOW

LATEST	EARLIEST	EVENT/ACTIVITY
....	....	Division officer ensure personnel working on evaluation input.
....	....	Division officer review/approve eval (forward for review as necessary)
....	....	Smooth type eval, proof read, and prepare for approving official's signature
....	....	Approving officer sign evaluation
....	....	(1) Division officer review evaluation with individual. (2) Individual sign evaluation. (3) Division officer retain/destroy desired material and forward official evaluation copies.

Encl (1)

GRADING/RANKING SHEET

Subj: INDIVIDUAL RANKING OF _____ WITHIN _____
                              (pay grade)   (organization)

FOR THE PERIOD ENDING _____ .

#	NAME	PERFOR-MANCE	BEHAV-IOR	LEADER-SHIP	APPEAR-ANCE	ADAPT-ABILITY	TOTAL POINTS
1	JONES	8	7	9	9	10	43
2	SMITH	8	6	7	9	8	38
3	BROWN	6	7	6	8	7	34
	etc...						

COMMENTS: _____

IN THE ABOVE SPACES, INDICATE BY NUMBER THE INDIVIDUAL MARK IN
EACH AREA AS NOTED BELOW.

4.0=10 3.8=9 3.6=8 3.4=7 3.2=6 3.0=5 2.8=4 2.6=3 2.0=2 1.0=1

NOT OBS=X (NOT COUNTED)

Encl (2)

_____
(SIGNATURE APPROVING OFFICIAL)

INDIVIDUAL INPUT SHEET

The Navy NAVPERS Form 1616/21 was instituted to afford enlisted personnel the opportunity of providing evaluators with information they wanted evaluators to consider at evaluation time. This form was constructed to have universal application on a Navy-wide basis. For this reason, some information that would be useful at a particular command or organization may not find its way on the form. By including all required information on the NAVPERS Form 1616/21 on a locally prepared individual input sheet, additional useful information is made available to the evaluator. A sample of how a locally prepared ENLISTED PERFORMANCE EVALUATION REPORT-INDIVIDUAL INPUT SHEET might look like appears on the following pages.

PERFORMANCE EVALUATION REPORT
INDIVIDUAL INPUT
(ORGANIZATION)

NAME (Last, First, MI)   RANK   DATE PREPARED

INCLUSIVE REPORTING DATE: From _____ To_____

The submission of this form is a means of ensuring that your personal accomplishments, achievements, and creditable activity, during the current reporting period, are brought to the attention of your reporting senior, through the chain of command.

The use of the information provided is discretionary on the part of the reporting senior. Upon completion of the report, this form shall be returned to the submitting individual.

PRIMARY DUTIES: Indicate in parens number of months assigned each duty.

Significant & specific job/project accomplishments (**PRIMARY DUTIES** only):

COLLATERAL DUTIES: Indicate in parens number of months assigned each duty:

Significant & specific job/project accomplishments (**COLLATERAL DUTIES** only):

Schools or classes completed, special designations awarded:

Training, qualifications, or professional developments achieved:

69

CORRESPONDENCE & OFF-DUTY EDUCATIONAL ACHIEVEMENTS:

CIVIC & COMMUNITY VOLUNTARY ACTIVITY/INVOLVEMENT:

AWARDS, LETTERS OF APPRECIATION, PROMOTIONS, etc.:

FUTURE SCHOOL OR DUTY ASSIGNMENT REQUEST PREFERENCES:

OTHER ACHIEVEMENTS, ACCOMPLISHMENTS, ACTIVITIES, OR EVENTS WORTHY OF CONSIDERATION. CONTINUATION SPACE FOR PREVIOUS BLOCKS:

_____
Signature

SECTION II

PERFORMANCE APPRAISAL DRAFTER'S WORKSHEET

Subj: PERFORMANCE APPRAISAL DRAFTER'S WORKSHEET

1. <u>Purpose</u>. To provide guidance on how performance evaluations shall be documented in narrative write- ups for enlisted evaluations AND officer fitness reports. This document addresses the performance evaluation in general and is equally relevant to enlisted evaluations and officer Fitreps.

2. <u>Discussion</u>. This directive has one principal objective: To ensure that performance evaluations document, in specific terms and in specific sequence, what an individual contributed directly to command mission accomplishment and the more broad Navy objectives. Evals and Fitreps must answer the questions: (1) What has the person done for the command? (2) What has the person done for the Navy?

3. <u>Action</u>. Performance evaluations shall be written in accordance with the following guidance.

    a. <u>General Structure</u>. Narrative write-ups will be structured in the following format and sequence:

    (1) <u>OVERVIEW</u>

        Summarizes the overall performance of the individual, and for top performers, provides a relative ranking. The first two or three sentences are the most important and should set the "pace" or "theme" for the entire evaluation.

(NOTE: SEE EXAMPLE OPENING STATEMENTS IN ANOTHER SECTION OF THIS WRITING GUIDE)

The first sentence is the precursor for detailed comments in subsequent sections. Supplementary comments on other achievements can be included in the next sentences. This section should also mention individual recognition received during the reporting period (awards, achievements, etc.).

(2) <u>MISSION ACCOMPLISHMENT</u>

This section documents individual achievements in primary and collateral duties related to mission accomplishment (i.e., what has the person done for the command?).

It is an error to feel that only those in supervisory positions can contribute directly to mission accomplishment. A good watchstander who is making progress in PQS qualification is contributing to operational readiness--an important factor in supporting mission accomplishment. Of particular importance are comments in the area of directing, counseling, and leadership. With more junior personnel, it is appropriate to base comments on potential if there has been no opportunity for direct observation. As a general concept, it is proper to use both actual performance and demonstrated potential based on observed trends, in officer and enlisted performance evaluations.

(3) NAVY OBJECTIVES

This section documents performance in the "high-vis" Navy programs such as retention of subordinates and other major Navy objectives that surface from time to time.

(4) MISCELLANEOUS PERSONAL TRAITS

This section includes anything worthy or necessary of comment which has not been included in the preceeding sections (military bearing, appearance, verbal expression, and the like).

(5) SUMMARY

A one-sentence "grabber" that summarizes the personal traits and growth potential. This section includes recommendation for future duty assignments, promotion, etc.

b. <u>Specific Guidance</u>.

(1) <u>HIT THE MARK</u>

Any "shortcoming" mentioned in the narrative should be significant, either in terms of performance or potential. People are not perfect, and evaluations are written relative to the "typically effective" person who requires an occasional reminder on personal appearance, some supervision, etc. If the comment is made that a person requires occasional supervision, that means he requires supervision over and above what one normally expects. The effect, then, is that comments on minor deficiencies are automatically magnified when they are included in the write-up. Also, evaluators should recognize the negative content of phrases such as: Willingly accepts responsibilities; duties assigned (as opposed to volunteering); normally; generally.

(2) <u>BE CONCISE</u>

A direct, hard-hitting write-up is better than an elegant one--concentrate more on content and specific accomplishments.

(3) <u>BE FACTUAL</u>

Quantify individual achievements when possible.

(4) <u>BE SPECIFIC</u>

A few phrases or sentences on individual achievements mean much more than paragraphs on billet description, command employment, etc.

"No meritorious act of a subordinate should escape attention or be left to pass without reward, even if the reward be only one word of approval."

JOHN PAUL JONES

(5) CONSIDERATION

Take into consideration the rate and experience level of the individual relative to the rate (and NEC) authorized for the billet assigned. If an E-4 is filling and E-5 supervisory billet, that deserves consideration and comment in the evaluation. The same is true of officers filling a more senior billet.

(6) PROPER GRAMMAR

Use proper grammar. If you are not sure, check it out or do not use it in the write-up. Remember, the evaluator will, in turn, be evaluated on his use and command of the English language.

(7) DO underline high or strong points/areas. Use paragraph separation or other indention practices to afford quick and easy access to desired information. However, do not use continuation sheets.

(8) DO NOT restate the description of duties in the evaluation narrative section. That space is too valuable to waste.

c. Drafter's Check List

Forwarding a Fitrep or eval with all the required information will save time, help "save face", and it will help get it done correctly. (NOTE: Navy requirements in this area change from time to time. At this writing, the following areas needed to be considered on at least some Fitreps or evals.)

(1) Appropriate "Recommendation for Promotion/ Advancement"

(2) Physical Fitness

(3) Equal Opportunity

(4) Interculteral Relations

(5) ADVERSE REPORTS (require special action, see NMPC INST 1611.1 or 1616.1)

(6) Report date starts day after ending of last report (verify leave and transit as required)

(7) Individual Input Sheet Received and Considered

(8) Special Qualifications, Schools, etc.

(9) Future Duty Assignment Recommendation

4. Each person should review the draft narratives he submitted after they are returned. Note what was

changed, added, or deleted and keep these in mind when drafting a narrative in the future.

5. An individual's first superior in the chain of command will initiate evaluation narratives and marks. Each subsequent superior will correct, rewrite (as necessary), and forward the evaluation, going over draft discrepancies or shortcomings with the subordinate. A copy of all evaluation drafts (unedited) will be forwarded up the chain of command along with the submitted evaluation. Remember, whether or not an intermediate senior re-works a draft, that person becomes totally responsible for the content and grammar of that draft once it is forwarded to the next superior.

SECTION III

INDIVIDUAL

PERFORMANCE

REPORTS

(IPRs)

Subj: INDIVIDUAL PERFORMANCE REPORTS

(IPRs)

Encl: (1) Individual Performance Report Form

(2) Individual Performance Report Samples

1. Purpose. To establish an effective program for reporting superior or substandard performance.

2. Discussion. Enlisted evaluations are the most important part of a servicemember's official record. Evaluations are used, in part, to determine eligibility for type of discharge, reenlistment, advancement, service school and duty assignment eligibility. It is important that superior or substandard performance be documented AS OCCURRING to assure it is not forgotten and that it is available for consideration at evaluation grading time. The following conditions and possibilities make it of paramount importance that superior and substandard performance be documented while it is fresh in memory.

a. Long periods of time between evaluation reports.

b. Individuals may transfer from one job to another or from one immediate supervisor to another one or more times during an evaluation period. Information not recorded is thus lost.

c. An individual's superior(s) may transfer during an evaluation period. Again, information not recorded is lost.

3. Action.

a. Procedures & Responsibilities. Any superior in an individual's chain of command should complete an IPR whenever superior or substandard performance is observed in a subordinate.

b. Examples of when an IPR would be appropriate.

(1) Official award received.

(2) OUTSTANDING or UNSAT at any type of formal inspection.

(3) Individual instances of superior or substandard job performance.

(4) Volunteering for special assignments or projects (noting the results achieved).

(5) Significant off-duty time donated to job (note if voluntary).

(6) OUTSTANDING or UNSAT appearance at quarters, or as noted during the performance of duty.

(7) Late/UA instances.

(8) On other occasions as deemed appropriate.

c. <u>Routing</u>. When an IPR has been filled out and signed, it will be routed through the chain of command up to the division officer. The division officer will determine if the IPR should be reviewed by other personnel. (Note: Routing may be altered to reflect particular organization.)

d. <u>Retention</u>. Completed IPRs will be retained in the Division Officer's Notebook until the individual reported on is being evaluated. At that time, the person preparing the initial evaluation write-up will remove the IPRs from the notebook, consider the documents, and include such information as appropriate in the evaluation. As a reminder, isolated incidents or minor infractions should not be included in an evaluation write-up. One case of being ten minutes late for quarters and one haircut reminder in a twelve month period is not serious enough to be included in the narrative of an eval write-up. ALL IPRs will be forwarded up the chain of command along with the evaluation write-up. Once the evaluation is completed and signed by the appropriate personnel, all IPRs within the reported timeframe should be destroyed unless some are being retained for other reasons.

| (ORGANIZATION) | | INDIVIDUAL PERFORMANCE REPORT (IPR) | | |

NAME	RATE	DIVISION/WC	DATE

PERFORMANCE

☐ **MERITORIOUS**　　　　☐ **DEROGATORY**　　　☐ **OTHER**

REMARKS

SIGNATURE OF REPORTING SUPERIOR	SIGNATURE OF INDIVIDUAL BEING REPORTED ON

Routing:
Immed. Supvr _____ LPO _____ CPO _____ LCPO _____ DIV. OFFICER _____

(ORGANIZATION)   **INDIVIDUAL PERFORMANCE REPORT (IPR)**

NAME	RATE	DIVISION/WC	DATE
A. B. SEAMAN	SKSN	S-1	5 JUN 19XX

PERFORMANCE

☐ MERITORIOUS   ☒ DEROGATORY   ☐ OTHER

REMARKS

SKSN SEAMAN WAS 15 MINUTES LATE FOR QUARTERS THIS DATE. (STATED CAR TROUBLES)

SIGNATURE OF REPORTING SUPERIOR	SIGNATURE OF INDIVIDUAL BEING REPORTED ON

Routing:
Immed. Supvr _____ LPO _____ CPO _____ LCPO _____ DIV. OFFICER _____

(ORGANIZATION)   **INDIVIDUAL PERFORMANCE REPORT (IPR)**

NAME	RATE	DIVISION/WC	DATE
W. T. HATCH	RM2	CR	1 MAR 19XX

PERFORMANCE

☒ MERITORIOUS   ☐ DEROGATORY   ☐ OTHER

REMARKS

PETTY OFFICER HATCH IDENTIFIED BY C.O. AS HAVING BEST PERSONAL APPEARANCE IN DIVISION AT C.O.'s PERSONNEL INSPECTION THIS DATE.

SIGNATURE OF REPORTING SUPERIOR	SIGNATURE OF INDIVIDUAL BEING REPORTED ON

Routing:
Immed. Supvr _____ LPO _____ CPO _____ LCPO _____ DIV. OFFICER _____

SECTION IV

PERFORMANCE

COUNSELING

SHEETS

Subj: PERFORMANCE COUNSELING SHEETS

a. <u>GENERAL</u>.

A Performance Counseling Sheet is to be used by division officers when a substandard trend is established by an individual, or when a major discrepancy is discovered which does not merit NJP under the UCMJ. A Performance Counseling Sheet may be used to give a final warning before NJP is recommended.

b. <u>ROUTING</u>.

Performance Counseling Sheets are to be routed through the chain of command to the Head of Department upon completion of the initial counseling session.

c. <u>RETENTION</u>.

The retention action covered in IPRs also applies to a Performance Counseling Sheet.

PERFORMANCE COUNSELING SHEET

NAME (Last, Initials)	RANK	ORGANIZATION	DATE

AREA OF COUNSELING

☐ Performance   ☐ Dress - Appearance

☐ Behavior   ☐ Tardiness - U/A

☐ OJT - Training Progress   ☐ Duties - Responsibilities

☐ Other (Specify) _____

REASONS WHICH BROUGHT ABOUT COUNSELING SESSION
(Give details, facts, specific dates, names, sequence of events, etc.)

SOLUTION THAT COUNSELOR AND COUNSELEE DEVELOP AND DISCUSSED TO OVERCOME THE PROBLEM(S) AND PRECLUDE FUTURE INVOLVEMENT
(Outline all solutions and indicate which one(s) individual freely elected.)

COUNSELEE'S COMMENTS

COUNSELEE'S SIGNATURE	COUNSELOR'S SIGNATURE

REMARKS/FOLLOW-UP ACTION

(To be completed ONE MONTH following original counseling session.
Outline all efforts indicating dates, names, progress, etc.)

OUTCOME: ☐ **Problem Resolved**   ☐ **Problem Persists**

COMMENTS:

Signature/Supvr	Date

KEY COUNSELING POINTS

- Point out to counselee that serious flaws in performance/behavior ARE considered as input information on Enlisted Evaluations.
- Counseling is performed to solve a problem or to fulfill a need.
- Determine interview objective prior to meeting, review available records, and arrange office seating for best results.
- It may be advisable for the counselee's immediate supervisor to be in attendance during the counseling session so that each will know exactly what is expected.
- Give the individual the facts, whether pleasant or unpleasant.
- Be a good listener - Be fair.
- Refer individual to more professional personnel if the problem can be better resolved.
- Follow-up on any new information brought to light during interview.
- Keep personal problems CONFIDENTIAL.
- Help the person to grow in self-understanding.
  DO NOT lose self control. The results could be disastrous.
  DO NOT make promises you cannot keep.
  DO NOT make snap decision.
  DO NOT forget to document the counseling and have counselee sign this sheet.

THIS PAGE LEFT BLANK FOR YOUR NOTES

CHAPTER THREE

EVAL & FITREP

FORMAT

&

SAMPLES

CHAPTER 3

PERFORMANCE APPRAISAL SAMPLES   PAGE

"Writing is an adventure. To begin with, it is a toy and an amusement. Then it becomes a master, then it becomes a tyrant. The last phase is that just as you are about to be reconciled to your servitude, you kill the monster, and fling him to the public."

WINSTON CHURCHILL

PERFORMANCE APPRAISAL

SAMPLE - INFORMATION

The performance appraisal samples in this guide are constructed in various styles and they contain the basic job accomplishment and potential format highly useful to selection boards. Navywide, however, many performance appraisals are seriously lacking in these two critical areas. There are three basic reasons why a large number of performance appraisal narratives do not contain a good, hard-hitting write-up similar to the ones in this guide:

1. Often times the evaluator believes that he is saying something helpful in a write-up (but is not);

2. Sometimes the evaluator doesn't know the difference between a good and a not-so-good write-up; and;

3. Sometimes the drafter feels compelled, because of today's inflationary marks trend, to grade someone high and then deliberately omit a hard-hitting narrative.

Whatever the reason, a person with "high" marks and a "low" write-up has less chance of being "passed" by a selection board than does a person with "high" marks and an accompanying "high" narrative. To the trained eye of a selection board member, the distinction is easy and the judgement is final.

The same work, or job accomplishment, can be committed to print in any number of ways. Some ways are better than others. The key is to remember to <u>write</u> <u>for</u> <u>and</u> <u>to</u> <u>the</u> <u>selection</u> <u>board</u>. All of the performance appraisal information and samples in this guide are excellent examples of how to write for/to selection boards in an impressive and favorable manner. The style, or technique, of writing to impress selection boards is easy to grasp. Note the 3-step initial draft format that follows, and then how that information serves as the basis for a strong, useful, and final performance appraisal narrative.

FIRST, RECORD JOB ACCOMPLISHMENT PARTICULARS.

For example: (from "Brag Sheet.")

-Maintained high percentage of equipment reliability.

-Corrected many long-standing material discrepancies.

-Graded high at material inspections.

-Excellent appearance of "troops."

-Good organizational recordkeeping abilities.

-Promotes high morale.

SECOND, LIST DESIRED "BULLETS" & "WORD PICTURE PERSONALITY" ITEMS.

Search through the "bullets" and "word picture personality" chapters in this guide and list those items that are appropriate.

THIRD, COMBINE THE FIRST TWO INFORMATION LISTS INTO DESIRED MIX.

PERFORMANCE APPRAISAL

SAMPLE - INFORMATION

Example (from previous pages):

"Possesses the spark of leadership, creative ability, and self-confidence to excel in any task. Despite being manned at 75% allowance, (name) was singularly responsible for maintaining equipment reliability at an amazing 98%, the highest in the department, throughout a six month period of high tempo operations.

During this same time his watch team:

-Completed 350 long-standing material deficiencies.

-Passed all zone/material inspections.

-Received a grade of "OUTSTANDING" at both command personnel inspections.

-Maintained operating logs and records in a thoroughly complete and up-to-date manner. Judged to be among the top two in the command.

Throughout the entire period morale and esprit de corps remained high and even flourished in this heavy operational period as each member of his team took a personal pride and sense of responsibility in their work. Initiative, accuracy, drive, and ability highlight his daily performance.

The "Brag Sheet" in Chapter 9 demonstrates how specific performance appraisal information can be collected during a reporting period. <u>All</u> top performers should maintain their own brag sheet.

The Sample Narrative Structure information on the following pages is a start-to-finish format and guide to use in constructing powerful, meaningful performance appraisal narratives. IT IS A SURE-WIN FORMULA.

PERFORMANCE APPRAISAL

SAMPLE NARRATIVE STRUCTURE

OPENING FORMAT

1st   note best attributes

2nd potential (for top performers)

3rd   awards and other special recognition received

JOB ACCOMPLISHMENT

- List specific accomplishments (use "brag sheet").

- Note "inner" personal characteristics on what possessed the individual to accomplish what was accomplished.

PERSONAL AND BEHAVIORAL TRAITS

List anything worthy or necessary of comment which has not already been addressed (behavior, appearance, etc.).

CLOSING FORMAT

1st   growth potential

2nd future duty recommendation

3rd   recommendation for advancement/promotion

A Sample Narrative Structure Form has been included on the following page. Copy that form, list on it the highlights of the information you intend to cover, and then use that sheet as a guide in constructing a smooth performance appraisal. The following pages take you through this procedure step by step. <u>The method is easy and the results are dramatic.</u>

SAMPLE NARRATIVE STRUCTURE FORM

OPENING FORMAT
1st Best Attributes

_____

2nd Ranking
3rd Potential
4th Awards

_____

JOB ACCOMPLISHMENT
Specific accomplishments
"Inner" characteristics

_____

PERSONAL/BEHAVIOR TRAITS
Behavior, Appearance, etc.

_____

CLOSING FORMAT
1st Growth potential

_____

2nd Future duty recommendation

_____

3rd Advancement recommendation

_____

SAMPLE NARRATIVE STRUCTURE FORM

OPENING FORMAT

1st Best Attributes	INDUSTRIOUS, VERSATILE ENTHUSIASTIC
2nd Ranking	2 of 10 in Department
3rd Potential	Virtually Unlimited
4th Awards	Letter of Commendation

JOB ACCOMPLISHMENT

Specific accomplishments
"Inner" characteristics

INNER QUALITIES: Skillful manager, firm but fair, adapts to change, good rapport with subordinates, gives personal and professional help.
ACCOMPLISHMENTS:
-Qualified ESWS/OOD Inport
-Outstanding at 2 CO's personnel inspections.
-Drafted & implemented 10 SOPs
-Developed PQS standards for 3 5-man department watch teams.
-Avg 97.25 on Command Inspection, 87.1 during Reftra.
-Excellent work as Repair Locker CPO

PERSONAL/BEHAVIOR TRAITS

Behavior, Appearance, etc.

Physically fit, plays sports Excellent use of English language--concise written reports & superior orator. Model of conduct & appearance.

CLOSING FORMAT

1st Growth potential	Ability to assume greater positions of trust and responsibility.
2nd Future duty recommendation	Instructor Duty/Command SCPO
3rd Advancement recommendation	Most strongly recommended

The above is a first draft example. The format is correctly set, items to be included in a performance appraisal have been noted. See the following page for a final draft narrative based on this first example.

SAMPLE NARRATIVE STRUCTURE (smooth)

Chief (name) is an industrious and versatile individual who approaches any task enthusiastically and with dispatch. He is a skillful manager with the proven ability to attain a high standard of performance in any endeavor. He directs his watch team with a firm but fair hand, and provides a unified purpose and sense of direction without dulling their initiative. Readily adaptable to changes in policy, procedure, or assigned workload, he always gives a personal contribution as a special effort to ensure cohesiveness and uniformity. He has established a good rapport with subordinates and does not hesitate to provide personal or professional assistance, when needed, and to encourage their trust through his genuine interest in their problems.

Chief (name) accomplishments include:

-Qualified ESWS in 9 months, and OOD Inport in 2 months.

-Received OUTSTANDING at 2 Commanding Officer Personnel Inspections.

-Drafted and implemented 10 SOPs. Excellent in content and enhanced operational effectiveness.

-Researched, developed, and implemented comprehensive PQS standards for his 5-man watch team. Standards proved so effective all three watch teams in the the department now use as guide.

-Division received grade of 97.25 during Command Inspection due, in large part, to Chief (name) organizational and technical abilities.

SAMPLE NARRATIVE STRUCTURE (Cont.)

-Watch team operational effectiveness graded at 87.1 during Reftra--highest grade in department.

-Received verbal and written praise from command DCA for the outstanding work and effort put into job as Repair Locker CPO.

A proponent of physical fitness, Chief (name) actively participates in various sporting events and maintains a trim physique. His conduct and appearance, on and off duty, are a model worthy of emulation by the entire CPO community. Well read; his written reports are clear and concise, and his oral presentations command the complete attention of a listening audience.

Chief (name) rare and successful blend of leadership coupled with his superior management and administrative abilities assure success in virtually any assignment. He stays with a job until it is completed, regardless of the time of day or night. During the past three months he worked over 100 off-duty hours reoutfitting and organizing a repair locker. Unlimited ability and potential. Highly recommended for Warrant Officer.

Chief (name) is ready for positions of increased responsibility and trust now. Recommended for instructor duty and for a billet as Command Senior Chief Petty Officer afloat or ashore. Chief (name) is most strongly recommended for immediate selection to Senior Chief Petty Officer.

PERFORMANCE APPRAISAL SAMPLE #1

Superior leader, manager, and organizer. Virtually unlimited potential. Continually supports and enforces command goals and policy. Mature, articulate, and dedicated, meets or exceeds all deadlines.

Accomplishments include:

-Reenlisted 7 of 8 eligible personnel.

-All personnel in (organization) qualified for advancement.

-Received Letter of Appreciation for outstanding work on, and support of, command 3M duties.

-Qualified OOD (Inport) in 3 months, OOD Underway in 6 months. Less than half average time. Runs taut watch team and enjoys my complete confidence and support.

-Excels in self-directing and self-pacing.

-Attains quality results at any tasking level.

-Uses penetrating and objective analysis in arriving at decisions.

-Chaired ad hoc committee on human resource manage- ment and development. Excellent results.

-Immaculate personal appearance.

-Cheerful, witty, and friendly, asset to high morale.

-Maintains articulate and up-to-date records.

-Active in community: Vice President PTA; Editor local VFW chapter newsletter; Church leader.

Unequalled ability to obtain maximum results of available material and manpower resources. Unyielding dedication and loyalty. Analytical in thought, reasoned in mind. Humane and compassionate. Works full day on operational matters and then dedicates off-duty hours to catch up on administrative matters. "Head and shoulders" above contemporaries.

(name) is a self-starter and inspirational leader. Seasoned counselor. Demanding yet fair, impressive leader and organizer. Strong moral fiber, respected by subordinates and superiors. Top achiever of boundless potential and ability.

(Recommendation for advancement/duty assignment.)

PERFORMANCE APPRAISAL SAMPLE #2

Industrious, meticulous, and accurate, (name) aggressively tackles any job. Unparalleled potential. Intolerant of mediocre performance, yet aware of personal limitations. Unhesitatingly offers constructive criticism when warranted. Subordinates are tactfully led to desired level of performance.

Accomplishments and strengths include

*Chairman of command Welfare and Recreation Committee.

*Led department to superb 89.2 grade on annual competitive operational exercises.

*Reviewed and made constructive recommended changes to three Navy warfare/operational publications.

*Maximizes strengths of subordinates.

*Encourages open, two-way communications.

*Positive influence in achieving command goals.

*Promotes working environment conducive to individual creativity.

*Achieves high quality results regardless of tasking level.

*Stimulates pride and professionalism.

*Excels in self and subordinate development.

*Unusually accurate, thorough, and effective in oral and written communications. Drafts smooth correspondence and instructions.

(name) optimizes available manpower and material resources. <u>Firm and fair</u>, an advocate of equal treatment and opportunity. <u>Flawless planning and execution efforts</u> virtually guarantee success of any job. Highly respected throughout chain of command for professional knowledge and personal professionalism. <u>Unbounded potential</u>.

(name) is a <u>proven leader, manager, and organizer.</u> <u>Unlimited potential.</u>

(Recommendation for advancement/duty assignment.)

PERFORMANCE APPRAISAL SAMPLE #3

(name) most productive and versatile (peer group) at this command. <u>Proven top quality organizer, administrator, and manager</u>. <u>Unlimited potential</u> for increased responsibility and authority. I awarded him a <u>Navy Achievement Medal</u> for sustained superior performance. Possesses <u>great deal of energy</u>, <u>highly industrious</u>, doesn't believe in idle time. Friendly personality, quick wit, establishes and maintains atmosphere of pride and professionalism. Partial listing of accomplishments includes:

*<u>Drafted finest organization manual</u> I ever read. 250 Page document was comprehensive, precise, easy to read. Dedicated 750 hours in construction, <u>500 were off-duty hours</u>. By request, copies given to other commands.

*<u>Constructed $150,000 budget</u> that allowed efficient and effective operations, yet employed financial restraint.

*<u>Qualified OOD (Inport)</u>. He <u>enjoys my complete confidence</u> and is highly capable of making independent judgement and decision.

*<u>Planned</u> and <u>coordinated</u> activation of command's...

*<u>Organized</u> and <u>tracked</u> 500-manday maintenance package with unqualified success.

*<u>Researched</u> action that updated 10 Naval Warfare Publications.

*Personally picked to conduct command LMET Classes.

*Conducted management workshops explaining requirement for proper recognition for superior performers and swift, humane, and just corrective action for substandard performers.

*EDUCATION: Completed 6 college courses during off-duty time with straight A average, and earned an Associate's Degree graduating with 3.74 GPA.

(name) fully enjoys Navy life, is quick to point out career benefits, and will not tolerate open dissent toward Navy or command policies or procedures. "Recruit Poster Quality" image. Poised and mature with thirst for knowledge and desire for challenge. Positive motivator, intelligent, and articulate.

(name) is a self-starter whose great personal initiative and leadership skills identify him as being "head and shoulders" above contemporaries. He runs an orderly and highly productive organization in any environment. Commanding presence, decisive, and determined. (name) has earned my strongest endorsement for immediate advancement and for promotion to Limited Duty Officer. Unlimited potential, of immense value to Navy--promote now.

(name) sets the standards by which excellence is measured. A proven manager and leader of unbounded ability. His superb working knowledge of systems and equipments has increased the operational excellence and capability of (organization) and was the basis for him being awarded a Navy Achievement Medal. He displays the character, initiative, and resourcefulness to accept and accomplish the most demanding tasks. The energetic and conscientious dedication he displayed in transforming his work group to a viable operating element within two months of assuming charge set the example--and pace--for the entire (organization). Reestablishing a quality control program that had been idle for some time was among his first priorities. Within 2 months he initiated a comprehensive test and control package that resulted in equipment availability percentages second to none. As tedious and demanding as this task was, he made time to assist in other important areas. His ideas and suggestions greatly assisted in developing new procedures to improve upon existing watch station qualification standards and contributed significantly toward a more effective administrative and operational environment. (name) is a self-starter. He took it upon himself to take charge of an inexperienced maintenance crew, identify numerous material and wiring deficiencies, and then executed a highly successful repair and upgrade program. That he has been capable and able to accomplish these and more tasks, individually and collectively successful, attests to his bold and imaginative leadership and management style.

(name) potential is unlimited.

(name) is especially adept in dealing with people. He understands the worth and dignity of each individual and successfully pursues a "follow me" leadership role. His demeanor, confidence, and spirit of cooperation have been highly commendable in many "crisis management" situations.

(name) is a dedicated professional who thrives on new challenges.

(name) is a dynamic leader and a superb manager. Ideally suited for top supervisory positions.

PERFORMANCE APPRAISAL SAMPLE #5

(name) is a dedicated, cheerful, and hard-working individual who performs all duties in an accurate and enthusiastic manner. Boundless potential. His ability to adapt to change and perform in a superior manner became quite evident during periods when he was called upon to assume several different billet functions. Never waivering, he accepted all responsibilities and challenges in stride, demonstrating versatility and exceptional managerial skills. Displaying a positive attitude, he has generated enthusiasm at all levels within the (organization).

(name) dress and grooming are impeccable. He always presents a neat and dignified appearance, reflecting obvious pride in self and service. Athletically inclined, he has been an active participant in a variety of command sponsored sporting events. (name) calm and affable manner are a prime asset in his daily coordination of activities. He always contributes full measure to any task and his willingness to accept added responsibility enhance his potential for positions of higher authority. He is quick to take the lead in coordinating activity and providing necessary guidance and supervision. Completely self-reliant, he strives for perfection and sees all projects through to their successful conclusion. Whatever the task or situation, he fully exploits the information and tools available to produce the most effective response. He gives fair and equitable treatment to all while ensuring the job at hand is done correctly.

(name) expresses himself excellently both in writing and speech. He is logical and direct in approach and factual in argument, making his points clearly and concisely.

(name) is a consistent top performer within his peer group, constantly seeking new and more effective methods in performing (organization) duties. He is knowledgeable of all methods and procedures within his area of responsibility and uses these skills as effective tools and guide lines in meeting all command tasks. (name) individual drive is motivating and refreshing. He believes in the Navy and its purpose, always upholding the highest tradition of the Naval Service. Unbound potential.

(name) is motivated toward a career in the Navy, and his devotion to duty and willingness to perform above and beyond what is normally expected mark him as an excellent candidate for increased and more demanding duties.

Recommendation for advancement/duty assignment.)

This special evaluation is submitted to recognize and document the all-around superior performance (name) has displayed throughout this abbreviated reporting period. <u>Unlimited potential</u>. He is an <u>exceptional manager and organizer</u> whose demonstrated expertise as a leader has <u>measurably improved the overall performance and readiness of this command</u>. An individual who <u>commands the fullest respect and support</u> of those with whom he works, he is <u>willing to accept any assignment</u> regardless of scope. He is an <u>original thinker</u> who has demonstrated the ability to devise and organize operational and administrative procedures that weigh time, personnel, and money while ensuring the most efficient and economic methods are applied to any task.

Some of (name) many accomplishments include:

-Reorganized the (organization) work schedule. His <u>superb administrative and managerial abilities</u> resulted in slashing 25% of originally scheduled man-hours required to (job). The job was completed within his time table without detracting from overall effectiveness.

-<u>Developed and implemented a training program</u> that attained remarkable results in minimum time. His (organization) went from 25% to 87% watch station PQS qualified in 2 months. In one month 3M PQS qualifications jumped from 45% to 100%.

-<u>Developed and implemented</u> 25 detailed, accurate, and well written SOPs. Much of this work was accomplished during normal off-duty hours.

-Received "OUTSTANDING" at two command zone inspections for the cleanliness and high state of preservation of assigned work spaces.

(name) is a self-starter whose work is marked by integrity and initiative. He is meticulously accurate with a great sense of responsibility for the quality of his work. A tireless worker, he cheerfully devotes numerous extra hours to ensure that all projects and problems are being taken care of and are followed through to a successful conclusion.

(name) accomplishments listed above speak for themselves. He is a true professional in every sense of the word. The courage of conviction and strong moral character he exhibits foster high morale, esprit de corps, and a total winning attitude.

(Recommendation for advancement/duty assignment).

(name) sterling performance noted in his previous evaluation has continued into the through this reporting period. Excellent potential. He has consistently executed the weighty responsibilities of the (billet) with fervor, determination, and overall superb success. Very talented...good sense of organization...a spontaneous propensity to leadership...a reputation for dependable and timely work. Strong and able in all areas, his most significant quality is his ability to impart his extensive operational experience and knowledge in subordinates.

Specifically, (name) was responsible for the following list of accomplishments:

*Streamlined record-keeping procedures which has noticeably eased the administrative workload and allowed primary emphasis on the operational mission.

*Revised operational techniques in (area) that led to a decrease in manpower requirements by 15 %.

*Updated logging procedures for (area), that ultimately led to one man being available for reassignment to a more operations-oriented billet.

*Developed a comprehensive PQS package for (billet). He spent upwards of 50 off-duty hours perfecting this package.

(name) has infused his (organization) with his enthusiasm and dedication. His astute management of personnel and equipment assets and his close attention to the material condition of his work spaces have markedly improved the operation, working conditions, and physical appearance of the (organization). (name) has proven that he is a tactful, yet strong leader by instilling in each subordinate the same desire to excel as he displays. The efforts and accomplishments listed above made a specific contribution to this command.

(name) is truly an exceptional (peer group). He is ready for increased responsibility now.

(name) is a "front runner" within his peer group.

(Recommendation for advancement/duty assignment.)

(name) is an outstanding (peer group). Unlimited potential for future growth and increased value to the Navy. He discharges all responsibilities with complete professionalism and tireless dedication. Ready, willing, and able are by bywords. Conscientious, tireless, and persevering. During most of this reporting period the (organization) has been involved in an extensive equipment/system modernization program. As (billet), he has had to manage around a myriad of problems not normally present in a strictly operating environment. This did not dull his enthusiasm or slow productive output. When the program commenced he worked well into the night on many occasions prioritizing an ambitious work schedule that made allowances for operational commitments without detracting from on-going maintenance and repair work. As a result of his sound leadership techniques and effective management, the project was completed three weeks ahead of schedule. Regardless of difficulties encountered, he always found a way to turn a potentially damaging problem into a short-term inconvenience. Throughout this demanding period he always received maximum support from subordinates because of his ability to generate enthusiasm through "follow me" leadership and direct supervision.

In spite of an already heavy workload, (name) found time to complete other noteworthy projects. They include:

*Maintained his organization's equipment in an operational, on-line status 98% of the time. Best in recent memory.

*Planned and implemented watch station PQS standards for 5 new operating positions.

*Reduced financial expenditures of his organization by 36% over those of his predecessor during an equal period.

(name) appearance and personal behavior are on par with his other exceptional qualities of performance. His records and correspondence are always correct and up to date and among the best in the (organization).

(name) is a proven leader and an accomplished specialist in his professional field.

(name) (organization) outstanding retention and advancement record, extremely low disciplinary rate, and the superior military bearing of his men are just a few examples of the positive indicators signaling his effectiveness and value to the Navy. (name) is recommended for promotion under the Navy's Warrant Officer Program.

PERFORMANCE APPRAISAL SAMPLE #9

(name) is a top performer. <u>Unlimited potential</u>. Totally <u>professional</u>, <u>poised</u>, <u>mature</u>, and <u>dedicated</u>.

Significant achievements include:

-<u>Awarded Navy Achievement Medal</u> for ...

-Awarded <u>Letter of Commendation from</u> ... for sustained superior performance during (period).

-Awarded <u>Letter of Appreciation</u> for off-duty assistance in civic functions.

Self-starter. Can plan, coordinate, direct, and finish job right the first time. Highlights of specific accomplishments include:

-<u>Established superb supply system</u> within (organization) that affords complete and accurate stock control management and auditing capabilities.

-(organization) Keyperson in Navy Relief, Combined Federal Campaign, and special Red Cross Drive. 100% participation.

-Drafted two command instructions and fifteen SOPs. All excellently researched, documented, and accurate.

-<u>Managed and led 15-man "tiger team"</u> in installation of new (equipment) and systems package. Completed three months ahead of schedule and $10,000 under budget.

Neat, trim, and fit. Immaculate "recruit poster" quality appearance. Articulate in speech, polite in manner. Submits timely and accurate paperwork. Enjoys loyalty, cooperation, and support of subordinates. Intelligent and dedicated, always volunteers for additional work to help shipmates and increase own knowledge, skill, and worth. A rising star of unlimited potential. Highly qualified and recommended for any demanding and challenging billet within or two pay grades above present rate/rank.

(name) does not believe in idle time or unfinished projects. Manages own time and that of others to best possible advantage. Possesses managerial and organizational expertise rarely observed in contemporaries. Completes large volume of work each day, frequently working extra hours.

(Recommendation for advancement/duty assignment.)

(name) performance, both militarily and professionally, is nothing short of outstanding. He has the potential to fill positions of greater trust and responsibility not normally available within the enlisted structure. Displaying a keen interest in his work, he sets and maintains a high standard of performance for himself and subordinates. He continually maintains a high state of operational and material readiness despite antiquated equipment and non-availability of spare parts and material support. Methodical and extremely conscientious, (name) actions are well planned, smoothly executed, and in the best interest of a job well done. In addition to his primary duties, he is a qualified ... Operations Watch Officer and is called upon to act in that capacity during personnel shortages. As expected of a man of his caliber, his watch team consistently produces quality results while being sensitive to the needs of command. He volunteered to assume responsibility for the command combined federal campaign, and as always, his enthusiasm infiltrated the command resulting in 97% participation and the highest dollar average per man in recent history. In the community, he is an active member of a Parent Teacher's Association and a coach for a little league team.

(Recommendation for advancement/duty assignment.)

Regardless of complexity or magnitude of the task at hand, (name) can be relied upon to see that it is completed expeditiously and efficiently. His high level of expertise is particularly exemplified by the in- depth, complete direction he provided the maintenance shop during overhaul. As a direct result of his guidance, complete equipment and systems were updated and refurbished to the extent that the level of dependability was equal to that equipment at the original time of installation. Not only a skilled technical specialist, he is also a dedicated leader whose standards of integrity and military bearing are of the finest quality. Under his direction, his spaces continually stand out at zone inspections with a sustained grade point average of 96.5%. The outstanding material condition of his spaces is totally impressive.

An accomplished counselor, (name) readily shares his experience with his personnel in both military and personal matters and they seek out his advice with regularity. He personally encourages every subordinate to set the highest possible goals for themselves and then counsels them on means available to realize those goals, both professional and personal.

(name) is highly recommended for the Warrant Officer Program.

(name) is one of the finest (peer group) in the United States Navy. His potential is unlimited. In his two years of dedicated service to this command he played a vital role in the the achievement of this command's mission and is a cornerstone of technical knowledge, management skill, and military tradition. I awarded him a Navy Achievement Medal for his work as (billet). His vast experience is enhanced by intelligence, sincerity, and ability to communicate effectively with all levels of command. Many of the improvements he either initiated or carried out have made their lasting mark on operations and administration within the ... Department. His intense dedication to duty, personal sacrifice, and uncompromising standards of conduct have provided the impetus for the organizational growth and development of the department.

(name) strong leadership, management acumen, technical knowledge, and personal diligence have resulted in the following specific achievements:

-Development of systems layout, standard operating procedures, and organizational design for the department.

-Efficient procurement and management of operational and administrative assets saved the command ... dollars in sorely needed financial assets.

-Brought the standards of military behavior and personal appearance in the department to the highest level through and intensive program of inspections, training, and personal leadership.

-Closely involved in the planning and implementation of equipment and manpower changes due to department consolidation.

(Name) is the most highly respected (peer group) assigned within this command. His total commitment to the Navy, support of his seniors, and leadership of those who serve under him have significantly enhanced readiness, retention, and morale. He is most strongly recommended for promotion to Limited Duty Officer. I would be pleased to have him as a member of my wardroom either afloat or ashore.

(Recommendation for advancement/duty assignment.)

(name) sets an exceptional example as a leader and manager. Virtually unlimited potential. He works a full day in his assigned job and consistently puts in many extra hours assisting in areas outside his normal area of responsibility. As a result, he has attained professional and technical knowledge and competence rarely observed within his peer group. The ability to obtain quality results in any environment and to relate to all age groups are the cornerstone of (name) success as a leader.

(name) displays a genuine concern for his fellow man, and he always finds time to help those in need of counseling and personal assistance. The emphatic demeanor and timely responsiveness he is known for has inspired and maintained high morale and team spirit throughout the department.

(name) ability to communicate his thoughts and commands, both verbally and in writing, is excellent. He is an exceptional orator, and his staff work is always timely and correct. Neat, trim and physically fit, he is a model of military bearing and Navy tradition.

(name) contributions to mission effectiveness include:

*Supervised a pilot program to test the effectiveness and feasibility of two new operational systems. The test was successful, in large measure, to the exceptionally efficient and methodical approach taken by (name).

*Implemented the operational phase of the equipment systems program with unparalleled success.

*Drafted 4 command instructions on systems test and operations.

Throughout (name) tenure as (billet), the innovative approach he displayed in day-to-day operations, as well as special programs, were consistently above the expected norm.

In summary, (name) has consistently performed all duties in an outstanding manner and has exhibited those traits that are highly desirous of a Naval (peer group)--strong leadership abilities; an excellent manager of material and equipment; tact and compassion; and, an innovative and intelligent view of the future.

Recommendation for advancement/duty assignment.)

PERFORMANCE APPRAISAL SAMPLE # 14

(name) is an intelligent, energetic manager and organizer. Enjoys fast-paced work environment. "Head and shoulders" above contemporaries with virtually unlimited potential. Quick thinker, makes positive decisions that are easily supported. Completely dependable, performs all tasks with accuracy and dispatch. Professional attitude radiates to subordinates, causing them to respond in kind with full effort and cooperation.

A sampling of (name) accomplishments include:

*Awarded Letter of Appreciation for suggestion on how to reduce equipment operation time when not on-line without detracting from operational capability. Suggestion will save Navy approximately $15,000 a year in reduced spare parts costs.

*Awarded Letter of Appreciation for work as Chairman of Command Welfare and Recreation Committee. As a direct result of his foresight, recommendations, and actions, command morale has been enhanced.

*Qualified as OOD (Underway).

*Drafted and implemented Department Regulations Manual. The 125 page instruction is complete, correct, and easy to read.

*Instituted many procedures that simplified and streamlined department operations and admin- istrative effort.

*Volunteered for collateral duty of Athletic Officer, and performed exceptionally well in that capacity.

*Active in command recreation activities, and serves as Vice President of local Parent-Teacher Association.

(name) has knack for getting job done where others fail. Informed on current Navy career programs. Information quickly passed on to supervisors who become highly responsive to needs of subordinates. Established routines which strengthened chain of command, facilitated smoother flow of correspondence, and created highly professional working atmosphere. Always a contributor to group effort. Works easily with seniors and subordinates. Sobriety, punctuality, and strong sense of duty highlight daily performance. Trim, physically fit, always "inspection ready."

(name) overall outstanding performance has contributed significantly to the high level of success achieved by this command.

(Recommendation for advancement/duty assignment.)

PERFORMANCE APPRAISAL SAMPLE # 15

Outstanding (peer group). Top notch manager and organizer. Well versed in all facets of technical specialty. Energetic and resourceful, plans ahead. Impressively managed (organization) transition from operating to overhaul environment. Structured organization meeting or exceeding all tasking. Devised highly effective management control system to track and identify delay or deficiency in shipyard or contractor work encompassing ... dollar, ... manday overhaul package. Subsequently identified and corrected various operating and design problems.

Accomplishments and achievements include:

-Managing ... manday ship's force overhaul and rehab work package. All major work ahead of schedule.

-Tracking and providing technical advice and assistance on ... SHIPALTS, including installation of (nr.) new equipments.

-Letter of Appreciation from (command) for personal assistance to that command.

-Drafted comprehensive ... page organization manual. Implemented and proving highly successful.

-Revised billet and training structure to better meet post-overhaul operational commitments.

-Excellent staff and paperwork--well researched, timely, and accurate.

-<u>Ambitious career counseling and training pro-gram</u>: 100% assigned personnel promoted from last two Navy-wide advancement examinations; 73% reenlistment record, first in the command; and, 100% completed off-duty college or self-study courses.

-Fit, tim, and erect in carriage.

(name) is a <u>self-starter</u> with <u>desire for challenge</u>. Has great deal of energy, doesn't believe in idle time. <u>Firm, fair unbiased leader</u>. Demands high standards of performance from self and subordinates. Effectively capitalizes on subordinate strengths and improves weaknesses. Enjoys fast-paced work environment. <u>Should be selectively detailed to demanding and responsible billets</u>. <u>Highly talented</u>, a <u>front runner</u>.

(Recommendation for advancement/duty assignment.)

(name) excels wherever assigned. He has proven himself an invaluable manager and counselor, and a source of knowledge and inspiration in every area of responsibility. Has capacity for higher responsibility. Early in this reporting period he was called upon to head a revitalized department training program. His response was immediate and decisive. Without waiting for guidance, he formed ad hoc groups to tackle the element problems he had observed. Each group was informed of what was ultimately expected, but allowed to approach their individual problem area as they saw fit, so long as the final result met desired goals. Within six weeks, an appropriate training site was secured, a short- and long-range curriculum was finalized, instructors had been trained, and the entire training program was off the ground five weeks ahead of schedule. In the first four months, 35 personnel completed the course, almost double the number expected.

Based on the strong managerial and leadership traits (name) displayed in his first major undertaking, he was subsequently assigned duties as Assistant Division Officer. Again, he proved himself up to the challenge. Administrative records were quickly brought in line with organizational policy; operating procedures were established and fed back into the training cycle; and, a new chain-of-command organization structure was devised and implemented with good success.

(name) tact, coordination, and his ability to get to the heart of any problem have increased the operational and administrative efficiency and effectiveness of the department. The impossibility of any situation does not occur to him. In addition to his other superb traits, he is an excellent counselor. His unique ability to reach a troubled person and give fair, honest guidance is without equal among his peers.

(name) is a dedicated Navy man of unlimited potential. He looks out for his men, yet requires each to give a full measure of productive work each day. The imagination, intelligence, and business-like manner he takes into each assignment virtually assures success.

(Recommendation for advancement/duty assignment.)

(name) is an extremely intelligent and dynamic leader with limitless potential. He is the top (peer group) in this command.

When (name) was assigned to his present billet, the department was faced with austere manning, antiquated operating procedures, and a core of untrained and unproven front-line supervisors. Never waivering, he quickly and accurately assessed the situation and immediately set out to generate solutions. By working with other divisions he was able to obtain administrative assistance to update operating procedures. Front-line supervisors attended up-to-date training sessions. (name) personally conducted organizational and managerial classes attended by his middle-manager cadre. Solid, proven leadership and management principles were highlighted and used as a foundation on which to build. The idea quickly caught on, key personnel began seeing the organization as a whole and their specific part in the operation. Suggestions started to flow up the chain of command from all levels. Many ideas proved effective almost immediately; some became effective after minor alteration; and, the suggestions without merit were quickly identified and discarded without undue delay. Within three months (name) had structured an organization that was dynamic in nature and allowed for self-evaluation and internal correction.

As a result of (name) initiative and professional approach: All deadlines began being met; morale improved dramatically; and, the total workload placed on each individual actually decreased as a result of people knowing what their job was, and what time-consuming, duplicating efforts could be jettisoned. Throughout this hectic time (name) displayed compassion and concern, and inspired unequalled loyalty and esprit de corps.

(name) is an asset to this command and the United States Navy.

(Recommendation for advancement/duty assignment.)

(name) performance continues to be underscored by pride, self-improvement, and accomplishment. Excellent potential. He was awarded the Navy Achievement Medal for superior performance at his previous command. His overall performance and dedication to duty are no less evident at this command. Initially assigned the primary duties of (job), he found time to assume other, equally demanding tasks. Filling in as the Department Administrative Assistant, he organized the monumental task of constructing a set of viable files and records following an extended period of inattention. In the area of training, he personally planned and scheduled the assignment of 15 personnel to 22 various schools. He made 3 no-cost TAD trips to various locations, ensuring necessary training was received and that NEC billets were filled within authorized limits. He volunteered to assume the increased and diverse duties of (job) when the person filling that billet was unexpectedly transferred. In this capacity he managed the successful efforts to meet all operational tasking. The job was particularly demanding and time-consuming with the department only 75% manned.

Working with others in a unified and cohesive manner is a particularly strong asset of (name). He has the ability to immediately establish and maintain excellent rapport with subordinates on all levels. Much of this is due to the fair, open, and unbiased manner he has in dealing with them. Each person knows that he will be given an equal opportunity, commensurate with capabilities, to work in any job or assignment, and that all will be given the opportunity to learn.

Eager to stay abreast of the latest changes in management, technology, and operations, he is currently enrolled in two courses at ...University, attending night classes. He recently completed three Navy training schools and two correspondence courses.

(name) is an achiever possessed with imagination and initiative.

(Recommendation for advancement/duty assignment.)

Superior ability and performance. Boundless potential. Exceptionally skilled in all facets of technical specialty. Totally professional and dedicated. Performance underscored by pride, personal involvement, and accomplishment.

Awards and accolades include:

-Navy Achievement Medal for superior performance as Project Manager of ...

-Navy Expeditionary Medal (period time).

-Message of Appreciation from TYCOM for professional assistance in ... Exercise as (job).

-Letter of Appreciation for community involvement in ...

Industrious and creative--an achiever. Likes to get into "nuts and bolts" of problems regardless of complexity or magnitude. Outstanding technical knowledge and managerial ability. Achievements and accomplishments:

-Identified equipment placement and workflow design discrepancies in ... operating spaces during major equipment reconfiguration project.

-Managing highly accurate progress flow charts and reference files on more than 75 command and contractor work packages. All ship's work progressing ahead of schedule and all contractor work on track due, in large measure, to (name) personal initiative, drive, and coordination efforts.

-Instrumental in revising department billet structure to eliminate administrative inefficiency and increase operational readiness.

-Educational interests: Completed three off-duty college courses through ... University pursuing ... Degree; and, completed six Navy correspondence courses.

-Able and highly capable administrator, submits smooth, well documented staff work.

(name) has unbound initiative and is extremely conscientious. Actions well planned, organized, and smoothly executed. Team player, fosters cooperation and harmony throughout command. A forceful, dynamic, and compassionate leader, knows how to motivate subordinates. Unlimited potential.

(name) is a head and shoulders performer.

(Recommendation for advancement/duty assignment.)

Unlimited potential. (name) sustained superior performance has been an inspiration to each member of this command. The deep respect and sincere affection he receives from all hands manifests his superlative qualities of leadership, integrity, and professional knowledge. His example has fostered unparalleled productivity and esprit de corps in the command despite severe cutbacks in personnel manning and significant organizational growth and reconfiguration. He represents the embodiment of pride and professionalism. These concepts are, and have always been, his benchmark as an advocate of tradition, loyalty, and a strong Naval Service. His outspoken support of the chain of command, firm enforcement of military standards, and equitable treatment of each subordinate has optimized morale and promoted effective mission accomplishment within the command.

(name) is never too busy to listen to a personal problem and is never reluctant to respond with positive action. His ability to anticipate potential problem areas or external factors which impact on current and future operations has resulted in timely compliance with all administrative and operational requirements.

He has distinguished himself through the following specific accomplishments:

a. Was selected and served with distinction as Chairman of the Command Welfare and Recreation Committee.

b. Played a key role in preparation for a command inspection. The command received high marks in all graded areas due, in large part, to (name) active involvement.

c. Brought all department administrative files up to date and participated actively in reviewing and updating command instructions.

d. Developed and implemented a personnel placement document, the first of its kind at this command. This resulted in a more effective assignment of personnel assets.

e. Developed performance standards for 5 administrative positions. The quality of these written standards was such that they have been used as models for other commands in the local area.

(name) unparalleled ability to manage money, material, and personnel place him number one in his peer group at this command, if not throughout the Navy. To highlight his abilities, he: -Builds on understanding and encourages feedback from subordinates. -Instills high-performance motivation and creativity. -Stimulates individual growth and responsibility.

In a word, (name) performance, across the board, has been nothing less than OUTSTANDING.

(Recommendation for advancement/duty assignment.)

Truly outstanding (peer group). Potential for positions of higher authority unlimited. Demonstrates unfailing diligence, job-aggressiveness, and total dedication to excellence. Thoroughly prepared for every assignment. Self-starter. Personal initiative and leadership skills guarantee exceptional results of all tasks assigned or assumed.

Top shelf organizer, manager, and administrator. Unique ability to assimilate myriad of diverse inputs and produce timely, accurate, and detailed results. Developed innovative management system to track manhours and work progress of all (organization) operations and management maintenance efforts. Experience, managerial abilities, and administrative talents were of immense significance in command earning ... Excellence ("E") Award, and grade of "outstanding" during Command Inspection. Constructed itemized $100,000 FY Budget which reflected most efficient and effective use of available funds.

Drawing on extensive administrative talents, (name) dedicated over 500 man hours of off-duty time constructing the most thorough, comprehensive, and precise Command Training Program package I have ever read. Accolades routinely received from senior attendees.

Poised and mature (peer group) with matchless thirst for knowledge and increased responsibility. Leadership, example, and skill in expressing views directly responsible for others seeking higher education. Always quick to point out career benefits. Directly responsible for persuading top performers to apply for officer and special enlisted education programs.

Erect in posture, trim in carriage. Qualified as OOD (Inport), earned my complete trust and confidence, most capable of making independent judgements and decisions required to run highly effective watch team. A strong performer during entire tour. A proven top achiever, demonstrates those specific talents and character traits required for ascent to positions of high responsibility.

(Recommendation for advancement/duty assignment.)

Extremely knowledgeable, industrious, completely resourceful (peer group). Performance of all duties singularly outstanding. Personally selected to assume division officer duties of a 75-man division for six months. Selected because of demonstrated superior management and leadership abilities. Division quickly and efficiently reorganized to meet increased operational tasking.

Exceptionally fine administrator. Superb ability to write clear, concise, and accurate material. All administrative matters submitted on time in smooth, ready for signature form. Originated incomparable division records in: General administrative matters; training; and, equipment management. Devoted literally months of intense off-duty effort and produced quality package that stands alone in sheer excellence. I have seen none finer.

Continually striving for personal growth. Completed three (under/graduate) courses, three Navy and one civilian correspondence courses.

(name) plans ahead, stays on top of every project or assignment until quality results achieved. Superb watch team leader, takes rapid, effective action without guidance from above. Excellent counselor, particularly adept in solving problems encountered by junior personnel. Unlimited potential for responsibility and challenge. All-around quality (peer group). Without reservation (name) has my highest recommendation for early advancement to (grade).

(name) is the Number One (peer group) in my command.

(Recommendation for advancement/duty assignment.)

(name) is an industrious, conscientious, and highly motivated (peer group) who exhibits the highest degree of professionalism in accomplishing all tasks. As (billet), (name) has been directly responsible for the outstanding performance of his undermanned (organization) as evidenced by the following specific accomplishments:

-Contributed personally to this command's mission during critical operations that lead to receiving ... Unit Commendation.

-Achieved equipment and systems reliability of 96.8%, despite heavy, taxing operations.

-Designed and completed major upgrade of obsolete wiring. The task was completed in half the allowed time, and without any loss of operational capability.

-Developed and implemented comprehensive Personnel Qualification Standards Program for the ... equipment. The first of its kind. Forwarded to TYCOM for use as a model.

(name) is an accomplished leader, manager, and organizer who has demonstrated the following personal traits and characteristics:

*Convincing speaker.   *Keen judgement.

*Meticulous administrative skills.   *Tireless worker.

*Inspiring leader.   *Tactful leader of subordinates.

*Informed and well read.   *Diplomatic personality.

*Alert, farsighted manager.   *Active, physically fit.

*Backs superiors and command policy.

(name) is a self-starter who has implemented many programs within his organization which have served to upgrade operational capability and increase morale. He served with distinction in collateral duties as: NJP Investigating Officer; HRM Instructor; Member Command Training Team; and OOD. (name) is an informed, concerned individual with a gift for getting along with others.   His advice is actively sought by juniors and seniors. Aware of need for effective communications, he successfully elicits continued high performance and morale from subordinates.

(name) is a bold, imaginative leader, ready for promotion now.

(Recommendation for advancement/duty assignment.)

(name) is an efficient and highly knowledgeable (specialty) whose performance, singularly and collectively, has been outstanding. Demonstrated unbound ability and capacity to successfully assume positions of greater authority and jurisdiction. Firm, earnest, exacting, and flexible. Although his (organization) is routinely undermanned 20-25%, (name) ensures highest degree of operational and administrative support while maintaining extraordinarily high morale. Shortly after assuming present position, he identified many equipment deficiencies and took corrective action as follows:

a. Identified and had 95 ... equipment deficiencies corrected within first two months, resulting in increased availability and reliability of equipment.

b. Obtained installed ... equipment which allows for real-time information and instantaneous reporting of operational evolutions.

c. Updated antiquated maintenance SOPs and procedures that reduced paperwork by 25%.

d. Measurably improved habitability of assigned work and living spaces.

e. Receives "excellent" or "outstanding" at all weekly zone material inspections.

(name) has provided outstanding operational support as well as continued superior administrative skills to various critical elements of this command. Adaptable, polished, and receptive, he is the man to see when a job needs completed with dispatch and efficiency.

(name) is a self-starter, confident of abilities and work. He volunteers to tackle any assignment without doubt or hesitation. Completely dedicated to Navy, its role and mission. Works zealously to complete each task as perfectly as possible. Possessed of a sound management background, the strong moral fiber of this (peer group) combined with an analytical mind and adaptability to changing situations makes him highly effective in any situation. (name) should be promoted ahead of his contemporaries and assigned to most demanding and challenging billets.

(name) enjoys my complete trust and confidence in any assignment, regardless of difficulty or complexity.

(Recommendation for advancement/duty assignment.)

(name) is an absolute top performer in every respect. His <u>outstanding leadership, superb management techniques</u>, and total dedication to duty place him <u>head and shoulders</u> above his contemporaries. <u>Unlimited growth potential</u>. Under his supervision and influence, every operational commitment was met or exceeded. His organization has received numerous expressions of appreciation from various commands for superior support. His (organization) consistently stood in the top two of twenty-five reporting stations for ... reporting excellence. Because of his overall superior performance he was selectively reassigned to the billet of ... His dedication and ability to get the job done regardless of circumstances were immediately evidenced. Within the first month, he received a personal <u>Letter of Appreciation</u> from (organization) for outstanding support and cooperation. He performs his many collateral duties with the same thoroughness and professionalism as his primary duty. As an OOD, (name) established himself as one of the top watchstanders in my command. <u>He has my complete confidence to represent the command in any circumstances</u>. Possessed of <u>quiet manner</u> and <u>commanding presence</u>. He displays total consideration for others in all of his endeavors, whether a professional or personal matter. These traits have earned him the genuine respect of seniors, juniors, and peers alike.

(name) is an <u>extremely well-rounded individual</u>. In addition to his demanding duty schedule, he actively engages in a wide range of off- duty activities. Specifically, he: Completed a two- week LMET School, one week of which he was on leave; actively participated in church and social activities, donating upwards of 100 off-duty hours working on community improvement projects; and, was the motivating force in organizing and managing various intramural athletic programs. (name) has demonstrated his potential for greater responsibilities through his uncompromising performance and professionalism. <u>He is the type of self-starting individual needed by our Navy in order to meet tomorrow's challenges</u>.

(name) is a model (peer group). He always adds more to the job than expected, putting it ahead of his own interests. He is <u>inquisitive</u>, <u>creative</u>, and <u>foresighted</u>. He consistently makes <u>sound management decisions</u>. An <u>energetic personality</u>, positive <u>"can do" attitude</u>, and <u>deep pride in his country and the Navy</u> highlight his daily performance. <u>Promote now</u>.

(Recommendation for advancement/duty assignment.)

CHAPTER
FOUR

WORD

PICTURE

PERSONALITY

SAMPLES

CHAPTER 4

WORD PICTURE PERSONALITY

INTRODUCTION

Documenting exactly what a person accomplishes in a performance appraisal is both useful and necessary. Work accomplishment alone, however, does not give a complete description or "picture" of an individual. The careful use of a few well chosen "word picture" adjectives can describe a person's inner qualities-- what possesses a person to do something, what a person "IS."

By combining what a person accomplishes and putting to print along with those accomplishments a person's personality characteristics, a complete "picture" of an individual is possible. Take, for example, the following:

"LT/Chief Jones is energetic, resourceful, and self-reliant. He (go on to list exactly what he accomplished)."

In the previous example, a selection board will know what was accomplished. More importantly, the board will gain valuable insight to the individual's "inner" qualities, capabilities, and potential-- *"energetic, resourceful, and self-reliant."* Selection boards do not promote people simply because they do a good job in their present pay grade. The potential to successfully discharge the greater duties of higher pay grades must be clearly in evidence. Potential must be documented in performance appraisals. Consider the following:

---

*Officers are not promoted because they are good division officers; they are promoted because they have the potential to become good Department Heads, XOs, etc...

*First Class Petty Officers are considered supervisors.

*Chief Petty Officers are considered managers. CPO selection boards do not promote good supervisors to E-7; they promote good supervisors with the potential to become good chiefs (managers).

By using the appropriate "word picture personality" characteristics listed on the following pages, selection boards can "see" and evaluate the full worth and potential (or lack thereof) of an individual.

WORD PICTURE PERSONALITY

JOB APPLICATION

The list of adjectives below express the emotional quality, the product of many factors, which manifest itself in the way the individual attacks and carries through his problems and duties.

FAVORABLE

active	deliberate	impartial	quick
adept	determined	industrious	rapid
ambitious	deligent	methodical	resourceful
aspiring	energetic	meticulous	skillful
boundless	enthusiastic	painstaking	thorough
competent	exacting	persistent	tireless
comprehensive	expeditious	precise	untiring
conscientious	flexible	punctilious	willing
			zealous

PERSONAL CHARACTER

The following list of adjectives express the inward traits of an individual and can only be learned after long and close association.

FAVORABLE

aggressive	faithful	inspiring	self-controlled
altruistic	firm	just	self-reliant
bold	forceful	loyal	self-sacrificing
broad-minded	forehanded	open-minded	sincere
cautious	foresighted	persuasive	stable
courageous	friendly	prompt	tenacious
determined	impressive	prudent	thoughtful
earnest	indomitable	resolute	time-serving

"An officer in carrying on his duty should be civil and polite to everyone, for civility does not interfere with discipline."

CAPTAIN THOMAS TRUXTUN

MENTAL OR EMOTIONAL TRAITS

The adjectives listed below express the outward qualities of an individual which generally denote possession of inward mental or emotional traits.

FAVORABLE

adaptable	generous	lenient	retiring
animated	good-humored	mild	serious
cheerful	good-tempered	pacific	spirited
cooperative	helpful	placid	spontaneous
cordial	humorous	quiet	tactful
courteous			

KNOWLEDGE

The following adjectives express the amount of subject matter an individual possesses, and NOT necessarily the ability to use it.

FAVORABLE

accomplished	enlightened	learned	well-read
astute	erudite	lettered	widely-read
brilliant	informed	scholarly	
cultivated	intellectual	well-grounded	

MANNER

The following adjectives express outward qualities of manner.

FAVORABLE

admirable	convincing	enterprising	pleasing
affable	cooperative	frank	polished
alert	confident	finished	quiet
amiable	courteous	friendly	receptive
animated	decisive	genial	reserved
assured	dedicated	gracious	restrained
benign	deliberate	kindly	retiring
bland	diplomatic	likeable	sedate
bright	discreet	magnetic	serene
calm	discerning	methodical	sociable
cheerful	dynamic	mild	suave
commanding	earnest	moral	tactful
compelling	eloquent	observant	tranquil
composes	engaging	persevering	unassuming
considerate		pleasant	straight-forward

INTELLECTUAL EQUIPMENT

The list of adjectives below express the type of, and ability to use, intellectual equipment.

FAVORABLE

able	careful	thinker	normal
agile-minded		ingenious	practical
analytical	clever	judicial	profound
apt	creative	keen	proficient
astute	discerning	level-headed	quick-thinker
bright	far-sighted	logical	quick-witted
brilliant	imaginative	mature	retentive
calculating	independent	methodical	remarkable

MENTAL FACULTY & CAPACITY

The following adjectives express intellect or intelligence.

FAVORABLE

acute	discernible	penetrating	thoughtful
alert	discreet	perceptive	witty
apt	farsighted	prudent	nimble
artful	foresighted	powerful	dexterous
bright	imaginative	quick	
brilliant	ingenious	rational	
clear-sighted	insightful	reasonable	
clear-witted	inspirational	sane	
clever	intellectual	sensible	
common sense	inventive	sharp	
comprehendible	judicious	sharp-witted	
conceptional	keen	shrewd	
conscious	knowing	skillful	
crafty	learned	sly	
creative	levelheaded	talented	
cunning	logical	thinking	
	mental	deductive power	

PRESENCE OR IMPRESSION

The adjectives listed below express the mental impression that an individual's outward qualities produce on others.

FAVORABLE

attractive	distinguished	neat
dapper	immaculate	sober
dignified	impressive	spruce
tidy		

JOB RESULTS

The following adjectives express the degree, kind, or type of results obtained by an individual.

FAVORABLE

accurate	decisive	excellent	sure
achievement	dependable	good	undeniable
beneficial	desirable	meritorious	unfailing
best	effective	notable	unmistakable
capable	effectual	reliable	unquestionable
certain	efficient	successful	unqualified
commendable	enduring	superior	

CHAPTER FIVE

EVAL
&
FITREP
BULLETS

CHAPTER 5

BULLETS

"We have too many high sounding words, and too few actions that correspond to them."

What is a "bullet?" A bullet is a statement that may or may not have a verb, object, or subject.

Bullets are straightforward, matter-of-fact statements.

Bullets have been used by some drafters of officer Fitreps for years. Today, Navy instructions recommend the use of bullets.

Bullets serve to reduce the amount of space required to make a statement. Thus, using bullets allows more material to be covered in the same space, or the same amount of material in less space, than formal sentence structure.

EXAMPLE OF FORMAL SENTENCE STRUCTURE:

"He is highly intelligent, possesses a stimulating imagination, and routinely provides sound advise and recommendations for anticipated problems."

EXAMPLE OF BULLET:

"Highly intelligent, stimulating imagination, provides sound advise and recommendations."

The samples in this chapter are in bullet form. They can be combined or used independently. The samples can be either shortened more, or they can be turned into complete sentences.

The sample bullets are broken into three basic categories to allow for ease of use in both officer Fitreps and enlisted evaluations. Although categorized into specific trait areas, many have universal application.

GRADED TRAIT

Category	OFFICER FITREP	ENLISTED EVAL
PERSONAL TRAITS	Judgement, Analytical Ability, Personal Behavior, Forcefulness, Military Bearing, Equal Opportunity	Initiative, Reliability, Personal Behavior, Human Relations & Equal Opportunity
MANAGEMENT & LEADERSHIP	Goal Setting, Subordinate Management, & Development, Work Relations, Equipment & Material Management, Navy Organizational Support, Response in Stressful Situations	Directing, Counseling Management
SELF EXPRESSION	Speaking Ability Writing Ability	Speaking & Writing Ability

BULLETS

ACTIVE/PASSIVE ATTRIBUTES

POSITIVE OR ACTIVE ATTRIBUTES	NEGATIVE OR PASSIVE ATTRIBUTES
1. active, energetic, quick & fiery, restless, athletic.	inactive, passive, slow & sure, steady and studious.
2. bold, aggressive, firm, just, forceful positive type, persistent.	timid, cautious, weak, negative type.
3. conceited, vain, cocksure proud and argumentative, insistent on rights.	unassuming, taciturn, unresponsive.
4. optimistic.	pessimistic.
5. patient, tolerant, pliable, easily turned, ability to admit own errors, lenient.	impatient, intolerant, stubborn, prejudiced, opinionated.
6. self-confident, intuitive, poised, no wasted motion, courage of convictions, power of decision.	lacks confidence, inclined to putter, becomes rattled, confused, hesitant.

POSITIVE OR ACTIVE ATTRIBUTES	NEGATIVE OR PASSIVE ATTRIBUTES
7. talkative, nervous.	quiet, calm,
8. radical, original, unorthodox, ingenious, resourceful, imaginative, experimental.	conservative, orthodox, convention-al, painstaking, lacks imagination.
9. courteous, tactful, considerate.	brusque, abrupt, hot-tempered, outspoken.
10. grasps essentials, not especially interested petty details. Observant.	slow to grasp essentials, falls back on details.
11. mentally alert, a good thinker, reasonable, well balanced, mentally coordinated, well informed, thinks ahead, quick perceptions.	mentally dull, not an orderly thinker, jumps to conclusions lacks mental coordin-ation, learns slowly.
12. versatile, interested in non-professional matters.	a plodder, one-track mentally, unobservant
13. inspires respect of juniors.	does not inspire confidence.

POSITIVE OR ACTIVE ATTRIBUTES	NEGATIVE OR PASSIVE ATTRIBUTES
14. works well under pressure.	may burn or crack under pressure.
15. pleasing personality.	colorless personality
16. good sense of humor.	lacking in humor, serious type.
17. willing to assume responsibility, self-reliant.	avoids/unwilling to assume responsibility

"BULLETS" - PERSONAL TRAITS

...Fully capable of meeting new situations head-on and applying himself in a highly resourceful manner.

...Highly cooperative, always willing to help, invariably a leader in conference or group discussion.

...Physically fit, possesses stamina to carry on in demanding situations.

...Possesses every basic attribute to excel. Capable and dedicated, achieves uniformly outstanding results.

...A continuing source of innovative ideas and positive contributions.

...Meticulously accurate with high sense of personal responsibility for the quality of his work.

...Capable, competent, and well versed in the mechanics of his duties.

...Erect in posture, wears uniform with great pride.

...Wins acceptance of his ideas through understanding and good two-way communications.

...Completes tasks on time and successfully, does not sacrifice quality for quantity.

...Drive, professionalism, and personal integrity have repeatedly earned highest praise from all quarters.

...Takes exceptional pride in image he projects, wears immaculate, inspection-ready uniform on daily basis.

...Patience, understanding nature, and ability to delve into the heart of a problem have earned great respect and rapport among subordinates.

...Analytical, decision-making ability, and adaptability to changing situations make him competent in any situation.

...Contributes full measure to any task, willingly accepts added responsibility.

...Work habits merit trust and confidence of others.

...An active listener, gets involved, grasps facts, feelings, and attitudes of others.

...Thoughts and actions spur results.

...Possessed with an unending urge--and ability-- to achieve.

...Relentless and energetic drive is inspirational.

...Exhibits initiative and resourcefulness in solving problems. Does not rely on outside advice or guidance.

...Employs personalized approach in dealing with subordinates.

...Understands worth and dignity of each individual, successfully pursues a "follow me" leadership role, both in his job and in his active enforcement of human equality.

...Mission effectiveness is enhanced by state of training and material readiness of his organization.

...Thoroughly familiar with all phases of his work and makes good use of this knowledge and experience whenever presented with problem or task.

...Motivated, concerned, and involved. Eager and interested in every facet of his job.

...Demonstrates boldness, couples with grasp of practicality, in attacking all responsibilities.

...Has total commitment to Navy and support of seniors and command objectives.

...Sound in judgement, eager, willing to accept added duties and authority.

...Positive, constructive, and creative in outlook. Plans ahead with great foresight.

...Adds more to job than expected, put duties, responsibilities, and desires of others ahead of own interests.

...Has stamina to tackle most difficult assignments, and the judgement and ability to obtain quality results.

...Devoted to duty and willing to perform above what is expected.

...Unswerving devotion to principles of equal opportunity.

...Highest personal honor, integrity, and intellectual capacity.

...Continually alert for ways and means to increase personal knowledge and professional growth.

...Dedicated, knowledgeable, and reliable in execution of all responsibilities.

...Works full day on assigned duties and then puts in extra hours assisting shipmates.

...Unflappable in backing chain of command goals and objectives, routinely gives shot in the arm to new projects.

...Response in stress situations always favorable and demonstrates his potential for high operational visibility jobs.

...Calm and affable nature are valuable assets in daily activities.

...Displays a relentless and energetic drive which has inspired and won plaudits of many.

...Highly innovative, atuned to changes, takes "crash projects" in stride.

...Successfully stepped into increasingly more difficult jobs with equally continuing success.

...Performance characterized by positive actions taken to meet growing responsibilities.

...Always contributes full measure to any task.

...Enjoys Navy lifestyle and is quick to offer positive advice to subordinates on ways to increase their worth and contribution to a team effort.

...Duties, across the board, have been skillfully performed.

...Physically fit, erect in carriage, squared-away uniforms.

...Technical competence and dependability have gained complete confidence of subordinates and superiors.

...A self-starter who can plan ahead, usually has most of a project laid out before formal tasking.

...Motivates personnel through personal and positive involvement.

...Readily offers constructive suggestions regarding matters outside his chosen technical field.

...Possesses inexhaustable drive and initiative.

...An ingrained respect for his fellow shipmate, secures high degree of loyalty and cooperation from subordinates, in whom he instills rare sense of personal responsibility for the quality of their work.

...Exemplary character, exercises mature judgement.

...Has meticulous military appearance, congenial personality, and positive attitude and outlook.

...Enjoys fast-paced operational environment, and is quick to lend helping hand to ensure cohesiveness and accomplishment.

...Aggressive in seeking out answers to developing problems and applying innovative solutions.

...A top achiever in any task assigned or assumed. ...Possessed of friendly, cooperative spirit and "can do" attitude.

...Deep concern for well being of others, total dedication and support to the Navy and the command he serves highlight daily activities.

...Decisions and efforts have contributed markedly to continued operational and administrative success of organization.

...Enjoys my complete trust and confidence in discharging all duties.

...Literally becomes personally immersed in programs and projects that promote high morale and camaraderie.

...Readily offers sound, constructive advice and suggestions on matters within and outside normal job with success.

...Possesses stamina, intelligence, and judgement to tackle any assignment and produce quality results.

...Daily and inspection appearance above reproach, highly professional military bearing.

...Applies excellent blend of common sense and logic when unforseen problems arise.

...Attacks each assignment with maturity, zeal, and determination.

...Follows through with verve and enthusiasm.

...Not satisfied with any performance short of perfection.

...Quick and innovative mind, always alert for new action.

...Sincere, easy-going, uncommonly likeable individual.

...Continually volunteers to shoulder additional responsibility.

...Ability to create and maintain confidence, respect, and professionalism in any organization.

...Excellent in attitude and capability.

...Timely and correct completion of primary and collateral duties has been exemplary.

...Personal involvement in management of training efforts stimulated professionalism and facilitated learning.

...Studious by nature, meticulously accurate as to facts, and thorough in work.

...Takes personal pride in appearance; shoes highly polished, uniforms pressed, and hair well groomed and short.

...Work is complete, thorough, and accurate; leaves no loose ends for others.

...Highly reliable and dependable in any situation, thrives on problems and situations which one of lesser ability and confidence would shun.

...Uncompromisingly committed to the principles of equal opportunity and fair treatment to all service members.

...Displays continued excellence and enthusiasm in the performance of duty.

...Unique ability to perform under pressure.

...Has the energy, initiative, and mental qualifications to tackle any assignment.

...Continually puts forth maximum effort in all areas of responsibility with consistently outstanding results.

...Knowledge of profession and job is impressive and desire to use experience in assisting others is commendable.

...Thoroughly meticulous in work and thought.

...Honest, sincere with unquestionable integrity.

...Widely read with retentive memory, continually seeks to broaden experience and increase professional knowledge.

...Gets satisfaction from doing rather than contemplating a completed project.

...Can be relied upon to take the initiative in implementing changes in policy or procedure.

...Ready wit and pleasing personality enhances morale.

...Dedication to duty in conjunction with desire to excel in any endeavor results in unusually high standard of performance.

...Repeatedly proven readiness to meet increasingly more responsible positions and challenges.

...Logical and direct in approach, factual in argument, tactful by nature.

...Confident of abilities, always one step ahead of the action.

...Personally aware of individual worth and dignity of subordinates and demonstrates awareness in daily interactions.

...Conscientious individual with excellent understanding and working knowledge of his specialty.

...Maintains impeccable personal appearance and commands similar high standards of subordinates, encouraging respect for Navy tradition and regulations.

...Alert, dynamic, highly intelligent with a creative mind.

...Encourages peers and subordinates to assume additional responsibility and authority.

...Continually seeks personal growth and development.

...Adapts quickly to changing operational situations and provides innovative solutions to stay on top of unfolding developments.

...Ability to express thoughts clearly and courage to stand on principle.

...A cornerstone of technical knowledge, management skill, and military tradition.

...Rapid, intense worker, produces accurate and timely results.

...Sense of fair plan and intense advocacy of individual and human rights.

...Devotion to duty, uncompromising professionalism and unflagging support of command and Navy goals.

...Vast experience enhanced by intelligence, sincerity, and ability to communicate with others.

...Intense dedication to duty, personal sacrifice, and uncompromising standards of conduct.

...Cultivates understanding, harmony, and esprit de corps.

...Confident of abilities, will take action when necessary without waiting for guidance or orders.

...Particularly effective in creating environment that makes subordinates want to seek career in the Navy.

...Stands above peers in terms of character, ability to get things done, and in demonstrated professional competence.

...Self starter, work is marked by integrity and initiative.

...Sobriety, punctuality, and strong sense of duty highlight daily performance.

...Enjoys fast-paced environment of job.

...Sincere counseling techniques secures complete trust and loyalty of subordinates.

...Attentive to detail, thorough and meticulous in manner.

...Has a good deal of drive and persistence and directs energy in attacking all tasks and projects.

...Positive "can do" attitude is infectious and enhances operational effectiveness.

...Performs duties with vision, judgement, and superior intellectual capacity.

...Well liked by subordinates, contemporaries, and seniors.

...Deep sense of pride and respect for Navy regulations and traditions.

...Readily adaptable to changing situations and demands.

...Has the courage of his convictions without being contentious.

...Imaginative, inquisitive, and creative, not content with old procedures and continuously explores new ideas with a view to improved effectiveness.

...Mentally alert, foresighted, thinks quickly on his feet.

...Displays patience in training inexperienced subordinates.

...Energetic self-starter with a warm, helpful, and alert manner.

...Actions and manners reflect creditably on Navy.

...Conceives and develops new concepts and procedures that result in significant improvements in (operations...maintenance...administration... logistics...management...training...leadership...).

...Resourceful in complicated or unusual situations.

...Exemplifies highest standards of moral integrity (deportment, or personal habits).

...Independent and perceptive thinker, recommendations have contributed appreciably to command's effectiveness.

...Poised and confident, maintains composure under pressure.

...Remarkable ability to adapt to requirements of superiors.

...Displays ingenuity in solving complex problems, or in devising temporary "fix."

...Superb facilities for effective personal interaction and leadership.

...Team player, places high emphasis on cooperation and team work.

...Frequently gives freely of off-duty time to work with subordinates to bring them up to his own high standards of efficiency and performance.

...A strong sense of duty and a desire to do a good job under any conditions or circumstances.

...Thinks clearly and logically and is able to accommodate and correlate a large amount of details in day-to-day duties.

...Facilitates communications and understanding between people with different points of view.

...Capacity to exercise high degree of imagination, ingenuity, and creativity is virtually inexhaustable.

...Atuned to his work environment, always one step ahead of the action.

...Strong personal belief in Navy traditions and customs.

...Instills pride in accomplishment, patriotism, and a sense of adventure.

...Strong desire and ability to be helpful outside normal area of responsibility.

...A student of human nature, displays social poise and tact (and: courteous, respectful, gracious, pleasant, frank, open-minded, even-tempered).

...Very diligent and invariably continues to work on a problem until every significant detail has been covered.

...Impartial, just, and ethical.

...Appearance is of "recruit poster" quality.

...Quiet individual with pleasing and poised personality.

...Enjoys fast-paced operational environment, quick to lend a helping hand.

...Demonstrates unsurpassed professionalism.

...Generates a spirit of harmony and cooperation.

...Proven performer under pressure and stress.

...Displays innate ability to coordinate myriad of details simultaneously.

...Has a polished manner, a keen sense of humor, and a personality that radiates enthusiasm even under adverse conditions.

...Self-motivated and resourceful, can be relied upon to complete difficult assignments without direction or guidance.

...Enjoys discussing the rewards and adventures of Navy life.

...Provided essential mission-ready support throughout the past year under most demanding and adverse situations.

...Highly proficient in all aspects of job, frequently used to train new managers and supervisors.

...Poised, can meet unusual and taxing situations without becoming rattled or confused.

...Has initiative, ideas, and aggressively follows through.

...Displays continued excellence and enthusiasm in performance of duties.

...Uncompromisingly committed to the principles of equal opportunity and fair treatment to all service members.

...An intense desire and ability to be helpful and cooperative.

...Thinks through problem areas and acts decisively on his own.

...Takes the initiative in seeking additional duties.

...Tactful, courteous, and well mannered.

...Meticulously accurate, with great sense of personal responsibility for every task, regardless of complexity or effort required.

...Fosters increased professionalism throughout ranks.

...Strong sense of dedication, moral obligation, and pride of rank.

...Inspects spaces frequently, knows what to look for, and results invariably bring about improvements.

...Even temperament and steadying influence instills sense of unity and pride of accomplishment.

"Damn the torpedos. Full speed ahead."
ADMIRAL FARRAGUT

...Approaches menial tasks with same enthusiasm and attention afforded major projects.

...Despite a high demand environment, remains calm and can be depended upon to render solid, logical judgements.

...Works quickly and efficiently, yielding results of the highest order.

...Energetic and logical with analytical thought process.

...Saved thousands of dollars through acute awareness, perseverance and personal diligence.

...A rare blend of personal candor, professional judgement, and self-starting motivation.

...Demonstrates a strong sense of dedication, wins support of subordinates and always achieves command objectives.

...Demonstrates remarkable ability to adapt to requirements of superiors, always putting the job ahead of personal desires, often at inconvenience to self.

...Work efficiently planned, completed, and carefully inspected.

...Ability to complete independent studies which can be used as guide for action by others.

...Knowledgeable and mature, uses communications as tool to arouse interest and enthusiasm of others.

...Exhibits personal and professional qualities that are prerequisite for personnel seeking greater responsibility.

...Shining example of proper dress and grooming.

...Ambitious and energetic, dislikes idle hands or mind.

...Demeanor promotes trust, efficiency, and high state of morale.

...Achieves high state of training and maintains high degree of readiness, and at same time attends to welfare and well being of subordinates.

...Is alert, ernest, and capable, and his attitude toward job ensure it is done correctly the first time around.

...Has totally mastered each and every professional, managerial, and leadership function within peer group.

...Actively solicits additional tasks and duties.

...Conduct and appearance always of highest caliber, demonstrates pride in self and service.

...Takes advantage of slack periods to pursue professional and personal goals.

...Maintains positive attitude and works well under pressure.

...Completes all tasks with alacrity and zeal.

...Meticulous in manner and attentive to detail.

...Very quick, but thorough, completing large volume of work each day.

...Frank, sincere, and honest in interpersonal dealings.

...Appearance is impeccable in either dress or work uniform, sets outstanding example for subordinates and peers.

...Maintains smooth flow of information up and down the chain of command.

...Hand picked for present job. Superior results support that decision.

...A high level of drive and energy, sharply focused to task at hand.

...Possesses well-rounded knowledge of Navy's latest career programs. Ideally suited to work today's young sailors.

...Maintains high standards for own performance and that of others.

...Energetic and dedicated, leads by example.

...Original thinker, ability to devise and organize procedures with maximum efficiency and minimum waste.

...Unafraid of accepting new and added duties, and has ability to produce quality results.

...Never loses capacity for enthusiasm and desire to help.

...Constantly learning, reads professional books and completes correspondence courses during off-duty and spare time.

...Sincere and outgoing personality is highly conducive to morale and fosters team effort and unity.

...Performs all duties with ease and confidence of a professional, attending to every detail.

...Dedicated, with an obvious willingness to serve with pride in any endeavor.

...A decision maker, develops plans and policies to attain goals.

...Consistently superior performer, totally dedicated to mission accomplishment.

...Ability to overcome obstacles and to secure cooperation from others on his own is indicative of ability to work independently and get the job done.

...Presents a neat, highly acceptable appearance in uniform and civilian attire.

...Exemplary character, exercises mature judgement.

...Uses available personnel and material resources with imagination and ingenuity.

...Straightforward in discussion, factual in presentation, persuasive and tactful in action.

...Readily tackles any job with intention and desire of mastering it--with unqualified success.

...Positive, constructive, and creative outlook.

...Grasps pertinent details rapidly.

...Not afraid of changing ways of doing business to eliminate those practices which drive good people out of the Navy, and to make a Naval career as attractive and satisfying an experience as possible.

...Development has been marked by meticulous precision in action and mature judgement in thought.

...A fantastic sense of humor and genuine interest in welfare and morale of others.

...Work produces results quickly and efficiently without organizational friction.

...Strikes effective balance between needs of service and needs of individuals.

...A self-starter with a natural ability and aptitude for technically oriented tasks.

...Sharp appearance evidenced daily, is immaculate. Uniforms reflect neatness in dress and attention to detail.

...Has sincere interest in welfare and self- development of subordinates and openly encourages-- and expects--professional and personal development.

...Rapid, thorough, and highly accurate in administrative and staff work.

...Completely competent in all technical and procedural aspects of chosen specialty.

...Positive, constructive, and creative in outlook.

...Displays aggressive work habits and an unending willingness to assist others in any capacity.

...Dedicated manager, positive and confident leader, maintains superior rapport at all levels of command.

...Possesses exceptionally valuable characteristics of soundness of judgement and eagerness and capacity to learn independently.

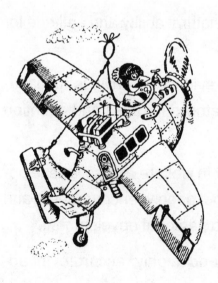

"The wise are instructed by reason; ordinary minds by experience; the stupid by necessity; and brutes, by instinct.

CICERO

...Exemplifies the spirit and pride and professionalism that is keynote of today's Navy: Industrious, reliable, adaptable to changing situations, and cooperative.

...Fit and trim in posture, takes great pride in maintaining high standards of personal appearance and demeanor.

...A disciplined mind with the ability to grasp and retain pertinent detail and information.

...Conscientious, punctilious, with a keen appreciation of responsibilities.

...Impeccable dresser, maintains very sharp appearance through personal physical fitness programs.

...Rare ability to create and maintain confidence, respect, and professionalism.

...Dedication, drive, and desire to put forth best effort in any capacity has increased operational effectiveness of this command.

...Thrives on pressures of immediacy and responds resourcefully with sound, innovative suggestions.

...Not content with idle time on his hands, seeks out solutions to any variety of problems during slack periods.

...Motivated, enjoys challenge, seeks personal responsibility, and is a high achiever.

...Places high priority on human goals. Generates spirit of equality, teamwork, and high morale throughout organization.

...Pleasant, pleasing personality allows him to both give and receive cooperation.

...Intelligent, stable, and possessed of an orderly mind.

...Dedicated with an obvious willingness to serve with pride in any endeavor.

...Attentive to responsibility, reacts decisively and positively to changing requirements.

...Concerned and humane, ensures each individual is treated with fairness and equality.

...Continuing source of new, innovative, and workable ideas.

...Possessed of a wide education and strong moral fiber.

...Charismatic and decisive, with good touch of common sense.

...Confident of abilities, will take positive and correct action when necessary without waiting for guidance or orders.

...Highly intelligent, possesses stimulating imagination, and routinely provides sound advice and recommendations for anticipated problems.

...Places high values on human goals and has adeptly integrated this feeling into dealings with others.

...Demonstrates persistence and conscientiousness in attacking any assignment.

...Remains calm when faced with situations aggravated by personnel shortages and new, untrained personnel.

...Steady and deliberate, compiled impressive maintenance record.

...Individual drive is motivating and refreshing.

...Possesses the mental dexterity and intellectual capacity to comprehend and tackle any assignment with unusual success.

...Pleasant in personality and reasoned in action.

...Smart, neat, and scrupulous in personal grooming.

...Deep degree of trust and respect accorded by co-workers.

...Cheerfully devotes numerous extra hours to ensure all problems and projects are being taken care of by following each through to successful completion.

...Amicable personality, spiced with good wit and humor.

...A "team player," places great emphasis on cooperation and coordination.

...Works methodically and carefully, and produces highly accurate results.

...Has a meticulous military appearance, congenial personality, and positive attitude which is demonstrated in daily contact with seniors and subordinates.

PERSONAL TRAITS

HUMAN RELATIONS - EQUAL OPPORTUNITY

(Words)

AMBASSADOR

AMIABLE

BEHAVIOR

BENEVOLENT

COMPASSION

COMPATIBLE

CONCERN

CONGENIAL

CONSONANCE

COOPERATION

CORDIAL

COURTEOUS

CREDITABILITY

CUSTOMS

DIGNITY

DIPLOMACY

DIPLOMAT

DISPOSITION

FEELINGS

FRIENDLY

FRIENDSHIP

GESTURE

GOODWILL

HARMONY

HUMANE

HUMANITARIAN

HUMANITY

IMAGE

INDIVIDUAL NEEDS

INFINITE PATIENCE

INTEGRITY

INTERACTIONS

INTERACTS

INTEREST

POLITE

RAPPORT

RESPECT

RESPONSIVE

SENSITIVITY

SINCERITY

SYMPATHETIC

TACTFUL

TRADITIONS

TRAVEL COUNTRYSIDE

TOUR

UNDERSTANDING

WORTH

"BULLETS"

MANAGEMENT & LEADERSHIP

...Fits each subordinate with challenging assignments, encourages self-esteem.

...Possesses professional competence to know what to do, fortitude to decide how to do it, and dynamic leadership to inspire others to accomplish it.

...Maintains highly accurate and easily understood methods of tracking and monitoring organizational work and accomplishment. Always knows what's planned and what's happening.

...Skillful manager of time, can quickly and efficiently diagnose problems and failures and supply effective remedies without delay.

...An informed leader who genuinely cares about the professional development and well-being of subordinates.

...A professional manager--understands principle of delegation.

...Mentally alert, with gift for devising organizational instructions and administrative procedure.

...Delegates authority effectively, does not run a one-man show. Delegation based on trust and mutual understanding.

...Morale never higher; yet, demands and receives full day's work from each individual.

...Goal oriented, demonstrates strong sense of duty and remarkable ability to plan, manage, and administer.

...Draws on abilities and strengths of subordinates.

...Is aggressive and initiates workable ideas for improvement of doing things more accurately, more quickly, and more thoroughly with the same means and resources as his contemporaries.

...Alert, with creative mind, able to develop effective and efficient procedural methods and prepare excellently written and easily understood instructions covering them.

...A student of human nature with superior ability to inspire cooperation from subordinates.

...Provides meaningful work assignments with which subordinates can identify and become personally involved.

...Has spiritual force and moral fiber necessary in a Naval leader.

...Possesses the spark of leadership, creative ability, and self-confidence to excel in any assignment.

...Highly flexible, adjusts management techniques to meet requirements of task at hand.

...Does not act before all facts have been properly evaluated.

...Executes excellent management practices by blending concern for others with job accomplishment.

...Thinks clearly and logically, able to accomodate and correlate large number of details in efficient and effective use of available manpower and material.

...Possessed of the vision, courage of conviction, moral integrity, and the capacity to inspire others to strive for excellence.

...Displays firm grasp and use of effective leadership principles.

...An original thinker, offers many new, innovative and well thought out ideas, many of which have been turned into policy and are proving highly beneficial.

...Made himself the "man to see" when subordinates need guidance of either personal or professional manner.

...Manages and controls use of maintenance equipment, including the more complicated and sophisticated, with unusual definition and precision.

...Ability to recognize potential of subordinates and provide the leadership to realize that potential.

...Genial, cooperative, with the courage of conviction.

...Possesses those special qualities it takes to be successful: He communicates easily; instills pride; encourages average performers to strive for excellence; and, commends people for effort, commitment, dedication, and personal accomplishment.

...Exerts personal influence over subordinates while allowing sufficient latitude for growth and creativity.

...Has capacity to make spontaneous and intuitive judgements of considerable value.

...Expresses himself with force and confidence. A real leader with a knack for getting the job done.

...Discusses strong and weak points with subordinates and takes sincere interest in improving their performance.

...Exceptional manager and organizer, ensures upward mobility of subordinates through carefully planning job enhancement and job enrichment programs.

...Strengthens morale by cultivating sense of well being and pride in belonging.

...A good listener, but will draw own final conclusions.

...Directs subordinates without dulling their initiative or deadening their interest or enthusiasm.

...Actively solicits junior personnel for their thoughts and ideas in variety of administrative and operational matters. Stimulates thought and action of others.

...Pleasant personality blends well in any work group, yet never loses sight of responsibilities as leader and supervisor.

...Consistently demands and receives only best from juniors.

...Organization functions smoothly, effectively, and reliably. Regularly meets commitments.

...Uses past experience, common sense, and excellent direct supervision to elicit most from subordinates.

...Balances schedule and workload according to priorities and produces quality results.

...A loyal, energetic, and conscientious leader.

...Introduces new ideas and encourages development of juniors.

...Encourages subordinates to put forth best effort, carefully explains advantages and rewards of self-improvement and a successful Navy career.

...Personified leadership by example.

...Straightforward but empathetic approach to subordinates with difficulties have resulted in quick resolution of many personal and professional problems.

...Masterful supervision and imaginative utilization of onboard personnel and equipment assets demonstrated on daily basis.

...Fair, impartial leader, respects rights of others.

...Inspires fullest cooperation and support of subordinates.

...Efficient organizer with sense of duty and desire to do a good job.

...Stands up for his men and they freely fall-in behind his able leadership and direction.

...Maintains awareness of changing situation, provides preventive rather than remedial management.

...Tactful, positive manner quickly gains respect and loyalty of subordinates.

...Grasps essentials of problem quickly, can think through a complex problem with rapid logic, aware of, but not distracted by, inconsequentials.

...Quick thinker who makes positive, supportable independent decisions.

...Motivates subordinates instead of driving them. They are eager to follow his lead.

...Demonstrated outstanding success as negotiator, arbitrator and group leader.

...Extremely quick to adapt to changing situations and never at a loss to find solutions.

...Individual of remarkable leadership talent and directional motivation.

...Impressively managed equipment assets and a maintenance work force and achieved high degree of combat readiness.

...Takes positive, decisive action in knotty situations.

...Every goal and objective met timely and correctly the first time around.

...A master at providing direction and leadership to junior personnel.

...Rare ability to apply corrective counseling and have it accepted in positive manner.

...Directs subordinates with firm but fair hand, providing unified purpose and sense of direction without dulling initiative.

...Backs juniors and allows to develop at rapid pace.

...Anticipates future tasks and through prior planning is never placed in position of pushing a deadline.

...Gets along extremely well, securing cooperation of contemporaries, and loyalty of subordinates, whom he guides and directs with understanding and tact.

...Exceptionally well qualified to examine existing organization and procedure to determine economy and efficiency.

...Directs subordinates by giving vision and purpose.

...Strong leadership, management acumen, technical knowledge, and personal diligence.

...Subordinates are best trained and most productive in the department.

...Excellent problem-solving facilities. Frequently emerges as chairman or spokesman in group activities.

...A dynamic leader, aggressive in job accomplishment.

...Ability to adjust to day-to-day workload variations while remaining atuned to overall priorities.

...Possesses constructive imagination necessary for unsupervised problem solving.

...Sells ideas and influences others with great success.

...Highly competent manager and administrator, with knack for passing own knowledge and experience to others.

...Has personal and professional interest in each subordinate. They respond by giving their "all" in tough and crisis situations.

...A knowledgeable individual of great foresight-- well prepared for any contingency.

...Ability to facilitate cooperative effort of others.

...Proven leader, capable of inspiring and motivating subordinates by demonstrating professional competence and by intelligent and compassionate treatment of subordinates.

...Proficiently exercises broad directive control over various tasks and projects simultaneously.

...Quick to take the lead in coordinating activity and providing guidance and supervision.

...Establishes climate that makes people receptive to his ideas and suggestions.

...Integrates mission requirements with individual needs and capabilities of subordinates.

...Clarifies and enforces unified action, challenges juniors.

...Works within well developed and defined long-range sense of direction and purpose.

...Initiated programs are designed to achieve maximum economy of funds and optimum utilization of materials.

...Has infectious enthusiasm that enlists cooperation and support of others.

...Never too busy to take time to teach and guide juniors, either upon request or when he observes additional instruction may be necessary.

...Ability to create enthusiasm for a given task.

...Demonstrates creative thinking and innovative problem solving techniques.

...An excellent administrator, will handle any job in highly creditable manner.

...Always busy, yet patient, sympathetic and understanding with subordinates who have problem.

...Definitely leader-type, has clearly demonstrated capacity for effectively and efficiently directing and controlling activities of others and for assuring high quality results.

...Ability to cut through confusion and conflicting information and get to crux of any problem.

...Has ability to succeed in multiple and diverse responsibilities with uncommon success.

...Ability to communicate effectively up and down the chain of command gained respect and admiration of juniors and seniors.

...Positive Navy attitude and personal application of distinctive leadership consistently inspired higher achievements from peers and subordinates.

...Fair and exacting, led by example and was always available to discuss better ways to accomplish a job.

...A master at achieving maximum use of limited resources.

...Astute on-scene leadership produced exceptionally positive results and maintained extremely high morale and a strong sense of purpose throughout (organization).

...A person of action who dynamically leads the way in setting and implementing command policy.

...Superbly carried out responsibilities to the distinct benefit of the command.

...Innate ability to anticipate problems and plan for their resolution contributed significantly to the enviable cohesiveness enjoyed by his organization.

...Always had time for his men despite heavily taxed work schedule.

...Initiative, drive and readiness to accept responsibility are proven to be without limit.

...Unique understanding of people, knowledge of equipment, and emphasis on training were key factors in (organization) ability to react positively to any situation.

...Managerial skills are of the highest caliber, and his aggressive and professional abilities clearly identify him as resident expert in (area).

...A role model for subordinates.

...Sound professional recommendations, base on experience and technical knowledge, are highly valued by superiors.

...Technical expertise, tenacity of purpose and enthusiasm are indicative of his pride and professionalism.

...Accepting his position of leadership, he rallied together divided factions within (organization) and focused their efforts, attention and energies on a common goal.

...Always provides superb performance under stressful situations.

...Rare individual who possesses maturity, intelligence, and technical knowhow to plan ambitious workload for himself and others, and leadership and dedication to successfully complete those assignments.

...Organization consistently maintained in high state of operational and material readiness.

...Maintains good work organization and disciplines subordinates competently and impartially.

...Has capacity to analyze facts, correctly understand and solve problems.

...Seizes every opportunity to promote the Navy and explain career opportunities and benefits. Open, friendly personality instrumental in gaining necessary respect to present Navy's career programs, with conviction, at formal and informal gatherings.

...Cheerful and cooperative, unassuming, fair and unbiased in exercising authority.

...Exerts personal influence with tact.

...Industrious manner and ability to get job done inspires trust and confidence.

...Maintains excellent blend between short-and long-term command objectives and accomplishment.

...Strengthens subordinate's feeling of belonging through personal commitment and involvement.

...Industrious and willing worker, extremely accurate in all that he does, placing great emphasis on detail.

...Engaging, good humored, and tactful and promotes good will.

...Stable and confident of abilities, readily and quickly adapts to changing situations.

...Intense individual whose paramount interest is in efficiency of his organization.

...Uses authority to assign and accomplish tasks in firm but fair manner.

...Great foresight, prepared for any eventuality.

...Recognizes potential of subordinates and provides necessary guidance to reach that potential.

...Consistently successful in obtaining complete and willing cooperation of others.

...Designed clear cut set of goals and moves toward them with initiative and purpose.

...Policies are prudent, in consonance with directives from higher authority, and implemented uniformly.

...Established a managerial and planning and control system that fully supported and enforced command objectives.

...Actively sought by subordinates for innate ability to get to the crux of a personal problem and help any concerned individual.

...Possesses direction of vision and economy of effort.

...Exercises high degree of imagination, ingenuity, and creativity in problem solving.

...Has progressive viewpoint with sound judgement; analysis of problems and choice of methods of accomplishing desired results are exceptionally good.

...Takes personal interest in supporting and developing professional attitude in subordinates.

...Instills self-confidence, uses incentives and reinforcement.

...Ability to achieve agreement among individuals and groups in furtherance of their common interests.

...Excellent planner and organizer, does not wait for instruction.

...Invariably submits timely and perceptive solutions to staff problems.

...Forceful without being overbearing and strict without generating resentment.

...Tactful and diplomatic, has ability to express and strongly support views on controversial subjects without arousing antagonism or resentment.

...Promotes harmony and fosters high morale.

...Exercises initiative, responds well to unusual situations or procedures.

...Displays superior administrative ability and managerial skill in organizing forces and planning events.

...Reinforces good behavior and corrects substandard behavior.

...Wit, charm, and vitality quickly wins acceptance in group efforts and puts him in driver's seat at gatherings.

...Observes chain of command principles, effectively delegates administrative and managerial responsibilities.

...Uses subordinates to best advantage, operates an efficient and productive organization.

...Fostered development from an embryonic state to a highly effective and responsive organization.

...An excellent manager and organizer who is willing to accept any assignment no matter how difficult.

...Especially adept at fitting people to jobs and training them quickly.

...Radiates confidence, composure, and competence.

...Ability to organize his time and that of others.

...Style of leadership designed to improve proficiency and morale of organization.

...Not naive or abrupt--uses tact and diplomacy.

...Strengthens morale by cultivating sense of belonging.

...Maintenance program is well organized and effectively executed.

...Competent and capable, leads by doing and showing.

...Discipline enforced on fair and consistent basis.

...Exudes spirit of well being and friendliness and improves attitude of all hands.

...Always open to inspiration and intuition, translates thought into action.

...Guidance to subordinates is clear and comprehensive. They always know what he wants.

...Ability to develop correct and logical conclusions.

...Takes sincere and persuasive interest in encouraging subordinates to improve their technical skill (or professional competence, resourcefulness, reliability).

...Commends superior performance and takes prompt corrective action in cases of substandard performance.

...Operates organization in climate that permits swift resolution of unforseen circumstances.

...Skilled in concentration and evaluation, has capacity to make spontaneous and intuitive judgement.

...Professional, accomplished administrator and manager who understands and effectively uses principle of delegation.

...Knowledgeable of Navy's career-oriented programs, especially school and duty station opportunities, provides good, sound advice on how to best take advantage of these options.

...Masterful supervisor with creative and imaginative use of on-board assets.

...Demonstrates skill in science of sound reasoning, valid deduction, and wise decision.

...Skillful manager, proven ability to attain high standards of performance.

...Establishes challenging yet attainable goals.

...A quick wit, good sense of humor, and easy going nature ensures amenable working relationships up and down the chain of command.

...Infectious enthusiasm enlists cooperation and support from others.

...Fosters prudent business management principles.

...Quiet in demeanor, tactful and thorough in positive handling of subordinates, quickly gains their respect and loyalty.

...Leads by doing and showing--a pace setter.

...Transfers goals and objective into concrete, workable plans.

...Intelligent, dynamic leader, thrives on new challenge.

...An excellent manager of personnel and equipment entrusted to his care.

...Day to day performance elicits positive and productive response from subordinates.

...Anticipates upcoming requirements and stays well ahead of rapidly unfolding situations.

...Has earned both abiding loyalty of subordinates and deepest respect of seniors.

...Professional attitude radiates to subordinates, causing them to respond with full effort.

...Establishes dialogue process with subordinates that enhances understanding and mutual respect.

...Ability to assimilate information and data and apply it to task at hand.

...Directs efforts of junior personnel toward quality work while promoting high morale and team spirit.

...Energetic and persevering by nature, anticipates future requirements and takes necessary steps to assure proper action ahead of impending deadlines.

...Concerned with well-being of subordinates. Maintains positive control and minimizes internal friction.

...An invaluable manager, counselor, and source of knowledge in every area of responsibility.

...Tact, concern for others, the "follow me" style of leadership elicits maximum effort and support from juniors.

...Always prepared for emergency procedures, ready for contingencies.

...Aggressive, but not overbearing, most effective in getting everything subordinates can give.

...Possesses decision-making facility that focuses on high issues and is action oriented.

...Displays excellent combination of tact and direct supervision, ideally suited to work with today's young, inquisitive sailors.

...Management effectiveness has set new standards of excellence in technical and maintenance performance.

...Manages his team of personnel with uncommon expertise, reliably providing scheduled services despite critical manpower shortages which, at times, called upon his wide range of innovative organizational abilities.

...Aware of changing situations, operates on preventive rather than remedial management.

...Has good judgement, common sense, and a sense of reality.

...An efficient organizer with a sense of duty and a desire to do a good job.

...Thinks clearly and logically and is able to accommodate and correlate a large number of details in the day-to-day management and leadership of available manpower and equipment.

...Decisions are always based on best available information.

...Possesses commendable faculty for getting projects started, keeping them moving, and accomplishing objectives.

...Thoroughly familiar with all phases of job and makes good use of this knowledge and experience whenever presented with a problem or task.

...Unwilling to be content to sit back and relax during slower periods of operation. Involves himself directly with training and furthering readiness, morale, and esprit de corps.

...Has good working relationship with subordinates and takes advantage of situations to inform them of Navy's continued need for knowledgeable and proficient career-oriented individuals.

...Ability to apply corrective counseling and have it accepted in positive manner.

...Possesses good judgement, common sense, and a grasp of reality.

...Ability to elicit the best of men.

...Balances schedule and workload according to required priorities.

...Engenders spirit in subordinates to do their best.

...Personable, well-liked and highly respected--continually exhibits outstanding leadership qualities.

...Has ability to create and maintain confidence, team work, and respect.

...Assumptions are logically derived from facts at hand.

...Bold, tempered with a grasp of practicality.

...Clearly demonstrated capacity for effectively and efficiently directing activities of others while ensuring high quality results.

...Good judgement, quick, decisive, and correct in action.

...Continually searches for ways to improve procedures and raise efficiency. Many suggestions incorporated at supervisory and management level.

...Outstanding manager, performs all duties without prompting.

...Gets subordinates involved in change and new ideas.

...Understands worth and dignity of each individual, successfully pursues "follow me" leadership style.

...Handles subordinates firmly and positively, but with such dexterity and tact to inspire a feeling of respect and devotion which assures a well done job in any assignment.

...Cheerful and cooperative, firm but unbiased in exercising authority.

...Quickly grasps essential elements of a problem, uses great initiative and keen logic in seeking solutions.

...Superior manager and leader, can distinguish between motivating and non-motivating forces. Takes maximum advantage of this rare quality.

...Highly qualified to teach subordinates the art and science of managerial and organizational techniques.

...A dedicated proponent of leadership by example, continuing education and training. Upward mobility in Navy is particularly evident.

...Ability to generate enthusiasm in subordinates and to instill in them a desire to do top notch work.

...Forceful and factual. Contributes to informal and formal group gatherings and meetings.

...Possesses ability to devise operational procedures that get job done properly and economically.

...Enjoys complete trust and confidence of subordinates while simultaneously practicing and enforcing strict adherence to established policy.

...Maintains high standard for own performance and instills, with success, this trait in subordinates.

...Organization enjoys high level of morale and a low infraction rate.

...Thinks out new ways and means to improve effectiveness with which a job can be done.

...Understands needs and knows capabilities of subordinates.

...Conducts frequent one-on-one informal discussions on future career opportunities of a Navy career.

...Established and strictly enforced highly effective controls on organizational materials. Reduced operating budget by ...%.

...Accepts responsibility and challenge in stride. Demonstrates versatility and exceptional managerial skills.

...Unique ability to solicit and receive full incentive and effort of subordinates.

...Realizes that people are most important and precious Navy resource and his leadership is highlighted by intelligent and compassionate treatment.

...Assertive yet considerate, leads by example.

...Personal leadership characteristics and tactful and understanding manner in which he handles subordinates secures their complete loyalty and causes them to exert every effort to earn his personal "well done."

...Carefully evaluates views of subordinates before making final decision.

...Informed leader with genuine concern for well being and development of subordinates.

...A "team player," highly cooperative with others.

...Firm believer in chain of command, keeps superiors and subordinates aware of changing situations.

...Highly talented with a good sense of organization, a spontaneous propensity to leadership, and a reputation for dependable and accurate work.

...Unwilling to sit back and relax during slow periods. Involves himself directly with training and furthering readiness, morale, and esprit de corps.

...Excellent working relationship with subordinates. Informs them of career opportunities and encourages self-development.

...Ability to devise operational procedures, and to write-up instructions thereafter in an intelligent and sensible manner so that they can be readily understood.

...Actively encourages individual growth and development of personnel, provides subordinates with definite, positive guidance.

...Extremely well organized, mission-oriented, and empathic with subordinates, has infused in subordinates his own enthusiasm and dedication.

...Strict, yet fair disciplinarian.

...Tactful and considerate of others, inspires mutual respect and self-confidence.

...Never too busy to take time to teach and guide subordinates, either upon request or when he observes additional instruction is necessary.

...Designs clear-cut goals and moves toward them with initiative and purpose.

...Mature thought process and sound logic used to arrive at valid conclusions.

...Places high importance on value of teamwork, fully realizing that without collective effort within and outside the department the command cannot fully succeed in mission.

...Uses authority to assign and accomplish tasks in firm yet fair manner.

...Strong leader, instills in subordinates same desire to excel as he displays.

...A "doer," a take-charge individual who is not content until all tasks have been completed correctly.

...Has ability to organize group work effectively, to properly divide tasks and allocate responsibilities, and to successfully correlate the various fractions of a job into one overall complete job.

...Personable, highly respected, exhibits outstanding qualities as a leader.

...Adapts quickly to changing operational situations and provides innovative solutions.

...Individual drive is motivating and refreshing. Masterful supervision and imaginative use of onboard assets demonstrated on daily basis.

...Does not hesitate to provide assistance to those in need and to encourage trust through genuine interest in personal and professional problems.

...Sets high goals and expects no less of subordinates.

...Original thinker, offers new, innovative ideas.

...Organizational practices stimulate sense of identification, belonging, and esprit de corps.

...Sincere, concerned, and honest leader, juniors frequently seek out his advice on personal and professional matters.

...Outstanding manager and leader, performs all duties without prompting.

...Encourages independent action, adds to productivity and efficiency.

Of the 18 U.S. naval victories achieved in the War of 1812, Commodore Edward Preble and "his boys" were responsible for 17. His motto, "Take care of your officers."

"BULLETS" - SELF EXPRESSION

...Drafts correspondence correctly. Reports and replies are prompt, thorough, and accurate.

...Well read and educated, correspondence is always precise and descriptive, conveying thoughts and concepts succinctly.

...Excellent speaker, can discuss wide variety of subjects with confidence and conviction.

...Commands large vocabulary which is used very skillfully and effectively in oral and written communications.

...Excellent writer whose reports, letters, and memos are well constructed and comprehensive.

...An interesting and convincing conversationalist--When he talks people listen.

...Capable speaker, interesting and convincing.

...Authoritative manner of speaking commands complete attention.

...Use of the English language is articulate, correct, coherent, and easily understood.

...An interesting speaker, and more importantly, a good listener.

...Meticulous and methodical in staff work.

...Articulate and persuasive, an excellent writer and orator.

...Communicates ideas in vivid, descriptive terms.

...Speaks in clear, concise terms that are easily understood by others.

...Continually demonstrates talent to communicate effectively with others throughout chain of command. Written reports concise and coherent.

...Expresses himself excellently both in writing and speech. Logical and direct in approach and factual in discussion, making points clearly.

...Written products clear and cogent, require minimum editing. Staff work on time and complete.

...Poised and ready, presents ideas in clear, easily understood manner.

...Written material always to the point, well researched and documented and ready for final print and distribution.

...Vivid and description in thought and presentation, either in written form or oral discussion.

...Exceptionally good speaker, presents ideas clearly and effectively and inspires confidence in the soundness of his views.

...Speaks and writes with great clarity.

...An excellent communicator with a ready and pleasing wit.

...Use of English language is articulate and easily understood. An interesting talker.

...Ability to express views clearly and concisely are of great value in group work.

...Uses correct grammar, spells and punctuates correctly.

...Interesting conversationalist, with ability to clearly and logically state views.

...Compositions are orderly and coherent. Sentences not lengthy or choppy.

...Exceptionally valuable in conference or group work. Expresses himself clearly and logically and his views are respected by those with whom he works.

...An articulate and persuasive writer and orator.

...Staff work is skillfully prepared and submitted in a timely manner.

...Clear in thought and direct in manner without being blunt in speech.

...A skilled communicator, able to express ideas accurately and precisely.

...Oral commands and written directives are concise, firm, and clear. They are readily understood and promptly executed.

...Reports are clear, concise, and convey desired meanings.

...Prepares skillful and timely reports, always prepared and up to date. Completes large volume of staff work each day.

...Excellent understanding of English language. Verbal expressions reflect self-assurance and poise, and writing is clear and concise.

...Has good and varied command of the English language. Written work reflects style characteristic of substance and content. Widely read.

...Authoritative manner of speaking commands complete attention of listening audience. Speaks in terms that are easily understood, but not shallow in content.

...Possesses varied command of the English language; is particularly adept at expressing ideas and thoughts in concise written form.

...Excellent in writing and speech, logical, direct, clear and concise.

...Good versatility in use of English language, enunciates well with excellent diction, and brief and concise in written communications.

...An excellent vocabulary and a clear, terse method of speaking and writing.

...Presents ideas in easily understood manner and written material requires virtually no editing.

...Highly accurate and professionally written reports have contributed in large measure to the high level of efficiency enjoyed by organization.

...Has innate ability to communicate clearly with his men, enabling his organization to function without confusion of purpose. Reports forwarded up the chain of command are equally succinct, exact, and graphic.

...Excellent ability to put thoughts into words, conveying both views and feelings with clarity and conviction.

...Expresses himself clearly and concisely. Speaks easily and straight-forwardly without undue repetition.

...Excellent vocabulary, uses correct grammar, good diction and enunciation.

...Speaks with good tone and inflection, voice reflects confidence.

...Persuasive in argument, sincere in expression, can gain and hold attention of others. A good teacher and instructor.

...Accomplished public speaker, either on scheduled or impromptu basis.

...Can develop and give good presentation to familiar or unknown audience. Thinks on his feet.

...Exhibits noteworthy talent for drafting smooth correspondence.

...Possesses good command of the English language, vivid and descriptive in oral and written communications.

...Has excellent ability to communicate clearly with his men, enabling him to provide for their needs both militarily and personally.

SELF EXPRESSION

DEFINITIONS

ACCURATE — Free from error.

ARTICULATE — Express oneself readily, clearly, or effectively.

CLARITY — Quality or state of being clear.

CLEAR — Easily understood.

COHERENT — Logically consistent.

COMMUNICATE — Convey knowledge or information.

CONCISE — Brief, devoid of superfluous detail.

CONVERSATIONALIST — One who excels in conversation.

CONVERSE — Talk, exchange thoughts and opinions in speech.

CONVEY — Impart or communicate by statement, suggestion, gesture, or appearance.

CORRECT — Conform to approved standards.

DICTION — Vocal expression; choice of words with regard to correctness, clearness, or effectiveness.

EDIT — To bring about conformity to written standard.

DEFINITIONS (Cont.)

EDUCATED	Having an education beyond the average; skilled.
ELOQUENT	Marked by forceful and fluent expression.
ENUNCIATE	To utter articulate words.
EXACT	Marked by thorough consideration of factual details.
EXPRESS	To make known opinions or feelings in words.
FLUENT	Ready in speech; polished.
GRAPHIC	Marked by or capable of clear and lively description.
IMPART	Convey or communicate.
KNOWLEDGEABLE	Having or exhibiting knowledge or intelligence.
LEARNED	Possessing or displaying extensive knowledge.
LINGUIST	One who speaks several languages.
ORATOR	One distinguished for skill and power as a public speaker.
PRECISE	Exactly defined or stated; minutely exact.

SELF EXPRESSION

DEFINITIONS (Cont.)

SUCCINCT	Compact, precise expression without wasted words.
SELF-EXPRESSION	Express oneself.
SCHOLAR	A learned person.
TERSE	Smoothly elegant; devoid of superfluous detail.
VIVID	Sharp, clear impression.
VOCABULARY	A sum or stock of words used or employed by an individual.
WIDELY-READ	Understand meaning of written word over a broad range.

THIS PAGE LEFT BLANK FOR YOUR NOTES

CHAPTER

SIX

UNFAVORABLE

EXAMPLES

CHAPTER 6

WORD PICTURE PERSONALITY

JOB APPLICATION

The list of adjectives below express the emotional quality--the product of many factors-- which manifests itself in the way an individual attacks and carries through on problems.

UNFAVORABLE

erratic	careless	casual
indifferent	indolent	intermittent
lazy	negligent	perfunctory
procrastinating	slow	sluggish
tactless	uncooperative	vacillating
unresourceful		

PERSONAL CHARACTER

The following list of adjectives express the inward traits of an individual and can only be learned after long and close association.

UNFAVORABLE

arbitrary	audacious	biased
bigoted	confused	dependent
disloyal	dominant	dominating
domineering	fickle	flaccid
hypercritical	idealistic	intolerant
irresolute	magnanimous	narrow-minded
negative	opinionated	prejudiced
selfish	superficial	timid
unfriendly	unstable	unsteady
weak	vindictive	

MENTAL OR EMOTIONAL TRAITS

The adjectives listed below express the outward qualities of an individual which generally denote possession of inward mental or emotional traits.

UNFAVORABLE

antagonistic	belligerent	complaining
conceited	evasive	excitable
fault-finding	gullible	hypercritical
ill-tempered	impetuous	impulsive
indifferent	indulgent	insipid
irritable	irritating	morose
naive	pessimistic	pugnacious
restless	resentful	spiritless
submission	supercilious	

KNOWLEDGE

The following adjectives express a degree of subject matter an individual may possess, but NOT necessarily the ability to use the information.

UNFAVORABLE

crass	dabber	dense
half-scholar	ignorant	shallow
smatterer	thick	unconversant
unerudite	uninformed	unscholarly
unlearned	unlettered	

Unfavorable bullets are deadly, use them carefully.

MANNER

The following adjectives express outward qualities of manner.

UNFAVORABLE

affected	aloof	blunt
boisterous	brusque	caustic
crude	curt	disdainful
dogmatic	frigid	inattentive
inconsiderate	indifferent	intolerant
loquacious	loud	moody
obsequious	obtrusive	offensive
taciturn	unresponsible	unresponsive

INTELLECTUAL EQUIPMENT

The list of adjectives below express a type of, and ability to use, intellectual equipment.

UNFAVORABLE

average	dull	formalist
impractical	inane	inept
mediocre	medium	obtuse
ordinary	perspicacious	second-rate
stupid	theoretical	undistinguished
unimaginative	unwise	

MENTAL FACULTY & CAPACITY

The following adjectives express intellect, intelligence, or in this case, lack thereof.

UNFAVORABLE

absurd	dense	dull
foolish	ignorant	inept
insensible	insignificant	irrational
obtuse	ridiculous	meaningless
senile	senseless	shallow
short-sighted	simple	superficial
trifling	unaware	uninformative
unintelligent	unlearned	

PRESENCE OR IMPRESSION

The adjectives listed below express the mental impression that an individual's outward qualities produce on others.

UNFAVORABLE

colorless	eccentric	floppish
odd	pompous	severe
slovenly	unattractive	undignified
undistinguished	unimpressive	untidy

JOB RESULTS

The following adjectives express the degree, kind, or type of results obtained by an individual.

UNFAVORABLE

adequate	below-par	commonplace
contradictory	defective	fair
faulty	inaccurate	ineffectual
inefficient	moderate	ordinary
passable	poor	presentable
questionable	second-rate	tolerable
undistinguished	unsatisfactory	worthless

PERFORMANCE WITH SHORCOMINGS

BULLETS

The following list of bullets are **UNFAVORABLE**. The sample write-ups following the bullets show how these bullets can be used along with some favorable traits to provide a complete performance appraisal "picture" of an individual.

...Lacking in cooperativeness and team work.

...Inclined toward stubbornness.

...Reluctant to accept responsibility.

...Produces only mediocre results outside area of specialty.

...Unimaginative and stodgy, best suited for routine jobs which are adequately covered by detailed instructions.

...Preoccupation with minor details frequently impairs soundness of judgement.

...Leadership capacity is limited and less than desired.

...Produces quality work only when closely supervised.

...Requires close supervision when working in (...) positions.

...Reluctant to make decisions in matters within scope of responsibility.

...Impatient in dealing with subordinates.

...Abrasive personality irritates others.

...Has little interest outside specialty field.

...Inexperienced and disinterested in administrative details.

...Overly methodical, slow to produce results.

...Requires constant (routine) guidance in determining what is major and what is minor in importance.

...Inclined to retain all responsibility and not give subordinates a chance to grow professionally.

...Lacks necessary persistence and conscientiousness to properly apply technical skills.

...Accepts suggestions of subordinates without proper evaluation of facts presented.

...Relies too heavily on others to give guidance and direction to subordinates.

...Is a perfectionist to an extreme.

...Inclined to overly berate subordinates when they fail to live up to expectations.

...Avoids any task or responsibility not directly associated with primary duties.

...Exhibits no desire to become proficient in management details.

...Has difficulty expressing views and opinions in writing (or orally).

...Should be selectively detailed and assigned to office and clerical duties.

...Sometimes takes more time than expected in performing independent tasks, being diverted by any number of personal interests.

...Has difficulty adapting to changes in policy or work conditions.

...Produces excellent work when closely observed and supervised.

PERFORMANCE WITH SHORTCOMINGS

SAMPLES

(name) is conscientious, honest, and thorough. He is, however, somewhat lacking in cooperativeness and is impatient in dealing with those who do not have his technical proficiency. Somewhat of a perfectionist with an inclination toward stubbornness, he at times irritates those with whom he works. He is reluctant to accept responsibility unless specifically assigned to him. He is positive in handling of his subordinates, but inclined to overly berate them when they fail to meet his perfectionist standards.

(name) is a highly qualified specialist in his field. However, he has little interest outside his specialty and he avoids, to the maximum extent possible, any task or responsibility not connected therein. On occasions, when he is forced to undertake duties outside his specialized field, he produces only mediocre results. He is both inexperienced and disinterested in administrative details, and has no desire to become proficient therein. He is recommended for duty in assignments where his specialty will take his time and is not recommended for duty where he must lead any number of men and manage large quantities of equipment.

(name) is sincere and thorough, though somewhat unimaginative and stodgy, he is best suited for routine jobs which are adequately covered by detailed instructions. Highly accurate and methodical in all that he does, he is a slow worker, but makes up for this by willingly working long hours. He has difficulty expressing his views, and his preoccupation with minor details frequently impairs the soundness of his judgement. He requires constant guidance in determining that which is major and that which is minor. Tactful and considerate of subordinates, he places little reliance on them, and is inclined to retain all responsibility himself. His leadership capacity is limited and less than that desirable of a person of his rate. He should be selectively detailed and assigned to office and clerical billets.

(name) has the manual dexterity and intellectual capacity to be an expert in his rating. However, he sometimes lacks the necessary persistence and conscientiousness to apply his skills. When assigned an independent task, he sometimes takes more time than expected, being diverted by any number of personal interests. Properly supervised, he produces good work, especially when working in technical areas. When required, he has proven he can adapt to changes in working conditions and policy. During the early part of this reporting period, he was not within Navy weight standards; however, after being placed on a controlled weight reduction program, he has recently reached requirements.

(name) is an intense individual whose paramount interest is in the efficiency of his organization. His loyalty, however, sometimes causes him to execute instructions implicitly, without perceiving that conditions may have altered the situation. Quiet, modest, and unassuming. Unselfish, generous, and idealistic to a fault. His enthusiastic interest in his organization and his idealism often cause him to accept the suggestions of his subordinates without proper evaluation of the facts presented. He requires close supervision when working in a management position, but when closely observed and guided he produces excellent results.

(name) is an industrious and willing worker, extremely accurate in all that he does, placing great emphasis on details. However, he is sometimes reluctant to make decisions in major matters within his scope of responsibility and relies on others for guidance and direction in those matters that represent departure from normal routine. Operating within a system of prescribed procedures with standardized and definitely specified methods and means, and spelled out functions and responsibilities, he secures positive and highly acceptable results. In the performance of duties under such conditions, he effectively controls and directs those workers for whom he is responsible, and insures that they produce desired results.

(name) is an excellent manager and organizer who is willing to accept any assignment no matter how difficult; he, nevertheless, leans to heavily on his subordinates and is too easily influenced by them, accepting their suggestions and recommendations with little or no analysis or consideration. An excellent conversationalist with a ready answer. He talks with force and finality though, on occasion, his answers, when analyzed, turn out to be "just words." He has a good sense of organization and an excellent administrative ability. However, his leniency in the management of his subordinates and the uncritical manner in which he accepts their work tends to reduce his effective value. This matter has been discussed with him, but he seems to be inherently reluctant to question or challenge the veracity and soundness of judgement of those who work for him.

THIS PAGE LEFT BLANK FOR YOUR NOTES

CHAPTER SEVEN

E-7, E-8, & E-9

SELECTION

BOARDS

CHAPTER 7

E-7 AND E-8/9 SELECTION BOARDS

PRECEPTS

Each selection board is given general guidance or instructions in the form of "precepts" by SECNAV, CNO, NMPC, and other Navy offices as appropriate. Standard precepts routinely include the following:

*Quotas for each rating are established by CHNAV-PERS.

*Candidates compete only with other candidates in their particular rating.

*Age and number of times competing for advancement are not considered.

*Being overweight will not stop a candidate from being selected for advancement; however, commands are required to withhold advancement until percent of body fat requirement is met.

*Pre-determined, specific career patterns and duty rotation are not established by selection boards. However, duty assignment experience and variation are considered.

*Each candidate must be fully qualified for advancement before he/she can be selected.

*Each candidate's record must reflect that he/she is capable of performing the duties of the next higher pay grade.

GENERAL INFORMATION

The voting membership of a selection board consists of a president (Captain) and officer and enlisted board members.

Prior to looking at a single record the board determines what subjects (evaluations, duty assignment, education, etc.) will receive advancement "points." Next the board determines the maximum amount of points that can be earned in each subject area. While one board may have a maximum point value of, say 750, another may max out at 1200. Regardless of the maximum value set by any given board, the weight factor percent on any subject remain relatively constant. That is, the board with 750 possible point could be expected to give approximately 400 points for evaluations (marks and narrative), or about 53% of the total points available. The board with 1200 possible points would probably give approximately 600 points for evaluations (marks and narrative), or about 50% of the total points available.

It can be noted at this point that evaluations are always the heaviest single weighted area. The Work Sheet Sample in this chapter lists generally accepted percentage values for individual areas or traits.

When subject areas and point or weight factor values have been agreed upon by the general board membership, a Work Sheet (or scoring form) listing subjects and point value parameters is constructed. The board is then broken down into small individual groups, with each group setting at a separate table. Each "table" consists of at least one officer and one or more master chief petty officers. Individual "tables" screen records of personnel in one professional area. A Boatswain Mate sits at a BM table, a Hospital Corpsman sits at the HM table, etc. If a particular rating is not represented by a master chief, that rating is screened by a table that has a closely related rating member. For example, if there is a QMCM on the board but no SMCM, the table with the QMCM would screen both the QM and the SM ratings.

Next, a board member takes a candidate's folder (consisting of a microfiche record, selection board brief sheet, and any correspondence received before or during the board's deliberation period), screens it, and transfers points "earned" to the selection board work sheet (or scoring form). A second board member then screens the same record and, using a separate work sheet, transfers points from the folder/record to the work sheet. If the two work sheets are consistent in total points awarded, the results stand. If there is any significant difference, the record is screened at least one more time. Table members go through each record in this fashion.

Upon completion of individual record screening, "slating" is accomplished by arranging candidates from top to bottom by numerical point totals. Quotas then determine who is above and who is below the "pass" line. As a general practice, the records of candidates whose point totals are just above or below the "pass" line are re-screened to assure point total accuracy.

Board members at the table must then agree on each candidate they are recommending for advancement. Next, table members become "sponsors" and "sell" each individual to the board's general membership via an oral brief, noting why a particular candidate is deserving of selection. The entire board votes on each candidate selection recommendation--majority rule.

Following initial voting action, the board then determines whether or not it is in conformance with special guidance precepts handed down by Navy officials.

WORK SHEET REVIEW

When reviewing the Work Sheet material on the following pages, keep the below information in mind.

Percentages are used on the Sample Work Sheet instead of actual point values. To equate what percentages mean in relation to point values, assume that 10 points equals 1%; therefore, 1000 points equals 100%.

When reviewing the work sheet, your first impression might be that the areas which award only 1 or 2 percentage points are not subject areas of strong concern. All areas deserve consideration and attention. Selection boards are looking for the "best qualified" candidates. In any given subject area some candidates are going to receive at least some of the points available. If you receive ZERO points in only 3 or 4 "minor" areas, that collective total of points "lost" is going to be very hard to make up in other areas. It is a good assumption that the candidates selected are going to earn points in virtually every subject area, and they are going to score high in the heavily weighted areas.

It is a fact that usually there are only a few points (perhaps less than 1 percentage point) separating the last name on the "selectee" list and the first name on the "non-selectee" list. No subject area can be conceded by a "front runner."

To see how your record would hold up in front of a selection board, go through it and award yourself points in each subject area. Grade yourself honestly and you can see where you need additional work. Think of all the people in your pay grade going up for advancement, give the person you rate highest in each graded area maximum points and then award yourself points based on that "ideal" maximum. Some weak areas can probably be improved upon by next evaluation period. Others may require careful planning (duty station variation and the like).

Areas/Traits listed under one particular heading in the following Work Sheet may appear under a different heading on another selection board work sheet. (For example, "Command/Community Involvement" is listed under the heading of "Potential." On another work sheet that area maybe listed under a separate heading. In either case "Command/Community Involvement" will be worth about 1% of the total points available.) However, the bottom line is the same; point values remain somewhat constant, regardless of what subject area a graded trait falls under.

THE **NAVY** IS NOT WHAT I DO.
IS WHAT I AM.

E-7 AND E-8/9 SELECTION BOARD

WORK SHEET OVERVIEW
(SAMPLE)

	MAXIMUM PERCENT	CANDIDATE'S POINT TOTAL
1. EVALUATION PERFORMANCE (31%)		
a. Overall Evaluation Marks.........	20%	
b. Peer Group Standing.............	6	
c. Leadership/Supervision Marks.....	5	
2. EVALUATION NARRATIVE (25%)		
a. Narrative Agrees with Marks......	10	
b. Job Accomplishment..............	3	
c. Accept Challenge/Responsibility..	3	
d. Managerial Ability..............	3	
e. Supervisory Ability.............	3	
f. Administrative Ability..........	3	
3. CAREER HISTORY (16%)		
a. Range/Variety Duty Stations......	5	
b. Range/Variety Jobs Held..........	4	
c. Sea/Arduous Duty Performance.....	4	
d. Special Qualifications...........	2	
e. Special Assignments.............	1	
4. POTENTIAL (16%)		
a. Early/Late Starter in Paygrade...	3	
b. Initiative......................	3	
c. Performance Consistency.........	3	
d. Volunteer Extra Work/Projects....	2	
e. Future Duty Recommendations......	2	
f. Advancement Recommendations......	1	
g. Problem Areas...................	1	
h. Command/Community Involvement....	1	
5. PERSONAL AWARDS (6%).............	6	
6. EDUCATION (6%).....................	6	
TOTAL	100%	

7. ADVANCEMENT EXAMINATION (E-7 ONLY) 4%
(4% taken from areas 1 through 6)

WORK SHEET BREAKDOWN

(SAMPLE)

1. <u>EVALUATION PERFORMANCE</u>

   a. <u>OVERALL EVALUATION MARKS (200 points)</u>

Breakdown Scale	4.00	200 Points
	3.98	195
	3.96	190
	3.94	185
	3.92	180
	3.90	175
	etc	
	3.80	150
	3.70	125
	3.60	100

   b. <u>PEER GROUP STANDING (60 points)</u>

Top Ranking Points (1 area only)

-Consistently Ranked Top/Nr. 1	50 Points
-Usually Ranked Top/Nr. 1	40
-Sometimes Ranked Top/Nr. 1	30
-Rarely Ranked Top/Nr. 1	20
-Once Ranked Top/Nr. 1	10
-Never Ranked Top/Nr. 1	0

Number Ranked Against

-Many	10
-None	0

c. LEADERSHIP/SUPERVISION MARKS (50 points)

Scale breakdown as noted for "OVERALL MARKS" above.

2. EVALUATION NARRATIVE

a. NARRATIVE AGREES WITH MARKS (100 points)

This area is a hedge against inflated marks. If very high marks are not justified in the narrative, a low number of points will be received in this area. Conversely, average marks and a good, meaningful narrative will receive extra points.

b. JOB ACCOMPLISHMENT

What was accomplished? How was it accomplished? Was accomplishment more/less than norm?

c. ACCEPT CHALLENGE & RESPONSIBILITY (30 points)

Volunteer/Ask for additional assignments. Was accomplishment more/less than norm?

d. <u>MANAGERIAL ABILITY (30 points)</u>

Demonstrated managerial skills, including areas of material, finance, time resources, and ability to plan and organize activities of others.

e. <u>SUPERVISORY ABILITY (30 points)</u>

How many people were supervised? Under what conditions? What were the results?

f. <u>ADMINISTRATIVE ABILITY (30 points)</u>

Administrative area is a mixture of:

-Administration: Paperwork, files, records, etc.

-Administrator: Includes managerial fringe areas.

3. <u>CAREER HISTORY</u>

a. <u>RANGE/VARIETY DUTY STATIONS (50 points)</u>

The more varied command assignments, and therefore the more varied command missions, the more points. A geographical spread is also helpful.

b. <u>RANGE/VARIETY JOBS HELD (40 points)</u>

The more varied jobs/duties the better.

c. <u>SEA/ARDUOUS DUTY PERFORMANCE (40 points)</u>

Sea duty includes duty stations that are considered sea duty for rotational purposes. What was performance at sea/arduous duty assignments?

d. <u>SPECIAL QUALIFICATION (20 points)</u>

Points awarded for special qualifications: OOD, ESWS, SS, Diver, Instructor, etc..

e. <u>SPECIAL ASSIGNMENTS (10 points)</u>

Includes duty assignments in following areas: Independent, isolated, embassy, instructor, recruiter, recruit company commander, etc..

4. <u>POTENTIAL</u>

a. <u>EARLY/LATE STARTER IN PAYGRADE (30 points)</u>

Comparison between performance when first entering a higher paygrade and later performance. (Which is to say: "Does it take time to "grow" into a higher position/pay grade?")

b. <u>INITIATIVE (30 points)</u>

Recognizing work that needs to be accomplished, and taking the lead in getting it accomplished without waiting for direction. This can include both command and community activity.

c. <u>PERFORMANCE CONSISTENCY (30 points)</u>

Sustained superior performance--all "peaks" and "valleys."

d. <u>VOLUNTEER EXTRA WORK/PROJECTS (20 points)</u>

Ask for more jobs/work, and perform well in those assignments. Work extra hours. Evaluation narrative should read "volunteered" versus "assigned."

e. <u>FUTURE DUTY RECOMMENDATIONS (20 points)</u>

Recommendation to fill special billets and billets of increasing responsibility and complexity: Instructor duty, Command Master Chief, and the like.

f. <u>ADVANCEMENT RECOMMENDATION (10 points)</u>

Recommendation for advancement in all evaluations. Strong recommendation? Recommendation for Warrant Officer/LDO?

g. PROBLEM AREAS (10 points)

Personal/Performance problems noted in an evaluation and not subsequently listed as being corrected/resolved...Or, no problems.

h. COMMAND/COMMUNITY INVOLVEMENT (10 points)

Serve on command boards/committees, be a Navy Relief Keyperson, etc.. Join community activities/projects..And, do more than just attend meetings; get involved and accomplish something.

5. PERSONAL AWARDS (60 points)

AWARDS (Examples)	Points Each
Navy Cross	20
Navy Commendation Medal	7
Navy Achievement Medal	5
Good Conduct Medal	3
*Letter of Commendation	2
*Letter of Appreciation	1

*Letters must be signed by approved senior officer ranks.

Unit awards (PUC, NUC, MUC, etc.) do not count.

6. EDUCATION

NAVY SCHOOLS: Points earned from schools vary depending of length, course content, type school, etc. Includes career counselor, instructor training, and job related schools. (Maximum 10 points)

NAVY CORRESPONDENCE COURSES: Both the number and the frequency with which completed are considered--looking for "sustained superior performance." (Maximum 10 points)

CIVILIAN EDUCATION:	Points (Maximum 40)
Each college course	1
1 Year College	10
AA Degree (2 years)	20
BA/BS Degree (4 years)	30
Masters Degree	40

7. ADVANCEMENT EXAMINATION (E-7 only) (40 points)

Not all E-7 selection boards award points in this area. When they do, highest test passer earn maximum and low test passers earn progressively less and less.

E-7 AND E-8/9 SELECTION BOARD

YOUR SERVICE RECORD

Does your service record reflect an accurate picture of you for the selection board? How the selection board views your record determines whether or not you will be advanced.

You should request a free copy of your microfiche record 3-6 months prior to selection board convening date. Include in the letter your full name, rate, social security number, and the complete address of where the record is to be sent. Don't forget to sign your full name. Telephone requests are not honored since your signature is required to have your record released. Allow 4-6 weeks for delivery. Submit written request to:

Commander, Naval Military Personnel Command
(NMPC-312)
Navy Department
Washington, DC 20370

If, after reviewing your record, you find errors or omissions, you may request the proper corrections. The record entry correction packet should contain all filmable documents which are missing from the master record. Send this material to:

Commander, Naval Military Personnel Command
(NMPC-313) Room 3038
Navy Department
Washington, DC 20370

To ensure that important information omitted from your record or any other pertinent information is presented before the board, a selection board packet should be sent directly to the appropriate board via certified or registered mail. Active duty personnel should mail the completed packet to:

President, (E-7 or E-8/9) Selection Board (ACTIVE)
Naval Military Personnel Command
(NMPC-221) Room 4631
Navy Department
Washington, DC 20370

If you believe your record was missing important documentation or contained errors that may have been reviewed during a selection board screening, write (via certified mail):

Commander, Naval Military Personnel Command
(NMPC-221)
Navy Department
Washington, DC 20370

THIS PAGE LEFT BLANK FOR YOUR NOTES

CHAPTER EIGHT

LDO & CWO

INFORMATION &

SAMPLE

WRITE-UPS

LDO/CWO
I EARNED IT

CHAPTER 8

LDO & CWO INFORMATION & SAMPLE WRITE-UPS

CWO - LDO ENDORSEMENT

WRITE-UP

As you read through the sample endorsements you may notice that many of them read somewhat alike. Selection boards have evolved to their present state over time. Proven methods of selection slowly give way to change, little by little. As a result, change from one year to the next is barely noticeable. So, too, proven ways of positively influencing selection boards change little from year to year.

Recent CWO/LDO selection boards have been consistent in their search for candidates who possess "proven" specific traits and characteristics. A good CWO/LDO endorsement write- up should encompass, either directly or indirectly, as many of the following areas as possible.

POTENTIAL	-For continued growth and value.
TECHNICAL COMPETENCE	-More so for CWO candidates.
EDUCATION	-A minimum of 60 semester hours college or AA Degree is practically a MUST for LDO. College for CWO is not mandatory, but is definitely helpful. In either case, the more the better.
DUTY/ EXPERIENCE	-Wide range/variety. Much arduous/sea duty.

LEADERSHIP   -Proven leadership in variety
                                   of jobs/ positions.

PAST SUCCESS   -Brief highlight in write-up.

SUSTAINED   -Brief highlight in write-up. Your
PERFORMANCE   record should speak for itself
                                   in this area.

INITIATIVE MOTIVATION ORGANIZER MANAGER

The above areas are directly related to well rounded "professionals." Selection boards are also looking for a "well rounded" person with high personal character and varied interests outside a strictly professional environment. While jogging, hobbies, and the like can be covered in your personal write-up, the command endorsement should convey the "whole person" in such areas as: INTEGRITY, RELIABILITY, MORAL STANDARDS, FINANCIAL/FAMILY STABILITY, and SOCIAL INVOLVEMENT/ACCEPTANCE (i.e. being a member of a PTA shows social involvement; however, being president, secretary, etc. shows social acceptance). Selection boards realize that when they promote someone to the officer ranks, that officer can stay around for years with only average performance. The board would obviously hesitate when asked to promote someone of "questionable" character.

LOCAL INTERVIEW BOARD

Some years ago an officer candidate was required to go before a Local Interview Board. Sometime in the mid-1970's this requirement went away. Now it is back. As long as there is a local board, candidates must do their best to favorably impress board members.

The questions board members ask are as varied and diverse as the members who sit on the board. There is no standard question list, each member is free to venture into any area he may choose. The variety of questions might range from, "If you saw a close friend of yours taking drugs, what would you do?" to, "What do you think about the United States' policy on (whatever)?" Local interview board members, for the most part, want your thoughts, ideas, and opinions on subjects. They are not looking for cut-and-dry "right" or "wrong" answers.

INTERVIEW BOARD HINTS

-Be straightforward, honest, and sincere (no B.S.).

-Don't talk too fast (or too slow).

-Don't talk with your hands (don't wave them around).

-Sit still, don't squirm around.

-Eye-to-eye contact. Use eye-to-eye contact when talking to board members. Don't look at only one individual. You are talking to the entire board. Share your eye contact with all members.

-Appearance. Must be above reproach from haircut to shoes.

-World events. Be prepared to discuss world events (watch the news on TV and read the newspaper--know at least what's behind the headlines.

CWO - LDO ENDORSEMENT

SAMPLE #1

1. Forwarded, strongly recommending approval.

2. (name) superior management and leadership abilities place him head and shoulders above his contemporaries. His work habits and "follow me" style of leadership have won the respect and admiration of his division, department, and the command. His exceptional administrative abilities have been sought for a variety of department and command projects, all with equally outstanding results. A cheerful, creative and industrious individual, he is, in every sense of the word, an "achiever."

3. (name) filled a division officer's billet in his first ... months at this command. During that time the command received numerous letters and messages of appreciation and commendation as a direct result of his efforts. Originators included: ..., ..., ..., and ... These achievements were especially noteworthy considering his division was continually understaffed by 20-25 percent of allowance. As a result of these and other accomplishments, I recently transferred (name) to a division where he relieved a LTJG as division officer. Within a month of his reassignment this command received a letter from ... expressing specific appreciation to (name) for his invaluable assistance in the indoctrination and training of their prospective ... Officer.

4. (name) honesty and integrity, coupled with his outstanding operational and technical competence, generates immediate confidence in his abilities by all with whom he comes in contact. His thoughtfulness, concern and compassion for all Navy members further enhance his strong supervisory abilities. He believes in the proper training and professional development of all subordinates is a matter of personal concern and prime importance, and he has adeptly integrated this feeling into daily division operations.

5. (name) ability to plan, coordinate and supervise the activities of others is second to none. He is a "head and shoulders" performer in the (peer group) ranks and I have every confidence in his ability to perform equally well as a (WO/LDO).

6. (name) is a proven leader who displays the technical knowledge, managerial ability, and constructive thinking required to perform exceptionally well as a (WO/LDO). He is ready for promotion now. I would be especially pleased to have him as a member of my wardroom now or in the future.

CWO - LDO ENDORSEMENT

SAMPLE #2

1. Forwarded, recommending approval.

2. (name) consistently performs in an enthusiastic and outstanding manner. Evaluations from previous commands indicate that he has continually maintained this excellent record throughout his Naval career. (name) possesses the ability to forsee and prepare for future needs as well as to act on present requirements. Utilizing his positive attitude and professional expertise, he engenders confidence in his subordinates, co-workers, and seniors. (name) outstanding military bearing is complimented by his no-nonsense approach to his duties, his constant awareness of his responsibilities, both to his organization and to his subordinates, and his personal appearance which is always impeccable.

3. (name) performance, not only as a leader, but in the wide and varied technical billets held, coupled with his extensive schooling and on-the-job training, indicates his potential for outstanding performance as a (WO/LDO) in the ... specialty field. He has demonstrated the attributes of determination, loyalty to the Navy, a mature sense of responsibility, and a pride of his work which exemplify the most desirable traits of an officer.

4. (name) has consistently displayed truly superlative performance in any assignment. His career pattern reflects strong and steady growth in every endeavor as evidenced by the numerous Letters of Appreciation and Commendation he has received for outstanding performance. In this command he has performed in three challenging, demanding billets requiring exemplary leadership and a thorough working knowledge of his rate. In his initial assignment as a ..., he performed in such a superior manner that he was selected for transfer to the ... Division to fill a Master Chief Petty Officer billet. In this much more demanding billet he was given a broad charter to improve operational readiness and the level of support provided to ... departments. His initiative and skill in devising new operating procedures dramatically improved the division's readiness and earned him the respect and admiration of all the command.

5. (name) is a top performer in the enlisted ranks and he has the potential to be a top performer in the officer ranks. (name) is highly recommended for promotion to (WO/LDO).

CWO - LDO ENDORSEMENT

SAMPLE #3

1. Forwarded, strongly recommending approval.

2. (name) is an outstanding performer in every respect. I have complete confidence, not only in his proven managerial and administrative abilities, but also in his maturity, discretion, and personal judgement. He is already performing at a level that I would expect from a (WO/LDO). He is a stand out (peer group)--a strong, positive leader, and an expert in his technical field.

3. (name) career as a ... has been broad and varied. He supervised watch section at ... and ... He has been Leading..., Department 3M Coordinator, Career Counselor, and Training Officer, and he is a qualified Inport OOD. His record confirms that his performance in these and other assignments has been an appreciable "cut above" the typical "good" performer. He is extremely well prepared to make the transition to (WO/LDO) in the ... community.

4. (name) has demonstrated a strong desire to improve himself personally and professionally. He recently completed requirements for an Associate of Arts Degree and is continuing his education, working toward a Bachelor's Degree. He maintains a stable family life and is committed to, and deeply involved in, a variety of civic and community affairs and projects. He is always in the thick of the action.

5.   (name) career shows strong self-motivation and an attitude toward the Navy that exemplifies the concept of "pride and professionalism." A proven leader who always obtains results surpassing command objectives and possessing a genuine desire for commissioned service, (name) is an outstanding candidate for selection as a (WO/LDO). I most strongly recommend (name) for immediate promotion to commissioned officer status.

CWO - LDO ENDORSEMENT

SAMPLE #4

1. Forwarded, most strongly recommending approval.

2. (name) is a "hard charger" who is an exceptionally talented and well-qualified candidate for commissioning as a (WO/LDO). He is a forceful, dynamic leader who knows how to motivate subordinates and get outstanding results. He is the best (peer group) in my command and I frequently seek his assistance to take on special projects, both operational and administrative in nature. Without fail, he has responded enthusiastically, with positive results, and ahead of schedule.

3. (name) is eminently qualified and prepared to accept the greater responsibilities and trust of a (WO/LDO). His career has been varied and he has held a number of increasingly more demanding billets and positions. The hallmark of all his past assignments is exemplary performance. He has an intense desire to excel in all endeavors. He is an outstanding candidate for (WO/LDO) in the ... Category.

4. (name) academic ability is best reflected in his completion of ... hours of college work, during off-duty hours, with an overall grade average of ... The scores of the correspondence courses he has completed range from ... to ... He consistently places at or near the top in all service schools. He always strives to improve himself and others around him.

5.   (name) has a cheerful, sincere, and professional attitude. He is always polite and courteous to his seniors, and is demanding, considerate, and imaginative in his leadership of subordinates. (name) believes in the Navy, is highly motivated toward a Naval career, and is an outstanding example for junior personnel to look to for guidance and assistance.

6.   (name) manifests the attributes most desired in an officer candidate. He is intelligent, versatile, highly motivated, and he continually exemplifies the highest possible standards of professionalism and performance. He is eminently qualified in all respects for advancement to commissioned officer status.

7.   The Navy needs men of (name) ability and potential in responsible positions. I would actively seek to have him assigned as a member of my wardroom, either afloat or ashore. I recommend him for promotion to (WO/LDO) in the strongest terms possible.

CWO - LDO ENDORSEMENT

SAMPLE #5

1. Forwarded, highly recommending approval.

2. (name) is an outstanding candidate for the Navy's (WO/LDO) Program. He is an energetic and methodical individual with the proven ability to excel in any assignment. His unique ability to immediately establish, and maintain, a close rapport and harmonious working relationship with today's young, inquisitive sailor led to his assignment as (organization) Career Counselor. In this capacity, he made significant improvements to the organizational structure and record keeping practices that ultimately led to improved effectiveness and an increase in first term reenlistments of 25%. He has been particularly effective in maintaining close liaison with the local Personnel Support Detachment to ensure that responsive support is provided and that all command requirements in the personnel area are met. (name) has the maturity to maintain the fine balance between mission requirements and concern for the individual, which is particularly difficult to define in administrative matters. As a result, he is exceptionally effective in dealing with subordinates, peers, and superiors.

3. (name) performance is second to none. He can be depended upon to accomplish any task presented to him

and on several occasions sacrificed his off-duty time to insure that a job was completed with utmost accuracy. As a supervisor and leader his professional and military competence is continually tested and has never been found lacking. His steady and uncompromising approach toward good leadership leaves no doubt in the minds of his men as to what is expected of them and makes following his lead an easy choice.

4. (name) academic achievements are truly impressive. Despite the disruptions of transfers while on active duty, he has aggressively availed himself of the opportunity to study and complete classroom and correspondence courses in order to earn a college degree. He recently completed all requirements for an Associates Degree and is expected to earn his BA Degree within the next year.

5. A complete professional and an outstanding example of the dedicated careerist needed in today's Navy. (name) is most strongly recommended for the (WO/LDO) Program. I would be particularly pleased to have him as a member of my wardroom.

CWO - LDO ENDORSEMENT

SAMPLE #6

1. Forwarded, highly recommending approval.

2. (name) expertise in the ... field has ranged from being an operator in ..., to a supervisor's job in ..., through a management position in a systems analysis and testing organization aboard a major combatant. His technical expertise, leadership, and management abilities far exceed those normally expected of a (peer group). These attributes, coupled with his rapid advancement through the enlisted ranks, are indicative of his desire and ability to accept positions of much greater responsibility. He is an outstanding candidate for selection to (WO/LDO) status in his first preference designator of ...

3. (name) is a top-notch leader, using an excellent blend of tact and direct supervision to elicit the maximum effort of subordinates. His correct appearance, military bearing, and flawless conduct project obvious pride in the service of the Navy and his country.

4. (name) has a goal of obtaining a BS Degree in Business Management. He has completed numerous courses leading toward attainment of his goal and is presently attending night classes with the University of ... His military schooling and Navy correspondence courses show extensive training not only for his rating, but in management as well.

5. (name) is a staunch supporter of the Navy and its career programs and he has been observed on frequent occasions discussing career reenlistment options with junior personnel throughout the command. He recently completed off-duty correspondence courses in the area of Navy Counselor to broaden his knowledge of, and gain insight into, these vitally important and rapidly changing subjects.

6. In my ... years of Naval Service, I have not seen a more qualified candidate for (WO/LDO). I would be particularly pleased to have (name) as a member of my wardroom, both ashore and afloat.

CWO - LDO ENDORSEMENT

SAMPLE #7

1. Forwarded, strongly recommending approval.

2. (name) demonstrates extraordinary professional ability, in depth technical knowledge, and uncommon perceptiveness in advancing the morale and welfare needs of his people while at the same time meeting all command goals and objectives. In recommending (name) for (WO/LDO), I am thoroughly convinced that he exemplifies those qualities and traits which merit his selection.

3. (name) is an exceptionally talented and well-qualified candidate who has consistently displayed superlative performance in a wide range of duties. His career pattern reflects steady growth in both technical and management skills, and he is the recipient of numerous Letters of Appreciation and Commendation for outstanding performance.

4. (name) ability to adapt to any assignment and his strong motivation toward self improvement indicate the potential for outstanding performance in diverse occupational fields within the officer corps. His self assurance, professional approach, and confident attitude make him an outstanding candidate for selection to (WO/LDO).

5. (name) academic ability is very impressive. His successful completion of a variety of military schools and correspondence courses attest to his desire to improve himself personally and professionally. Additionally, his selection of correspondence courses has been geared toward more fully preparing himself for advancement to commissioned officer.

6. (name) is fully qualified in all respects and will perform extremely well as a (WO/LDO) in the ... Category. He possesses the technical ability, administrative talent, mental acuity, and self-confidence to carry out all duties to which he may be assigned.

7. (name) is highly qualified for appointment to the (WO/LDO) Program, and he is strongly recommended for selection.

CWO - LDO ENDORSEMENT

SAMPLE #8

1. Forwarded, highly recommending approval.

2. (name) is an excellent candidate for (WO/LDO). His ability to organize and make correct decisions is outstanding. His professional knowledge, technical competence and attention to detail is impressive. His supervisory ability, demonstrated by his rapport with subordinates and work accomplishment, is excellent.

3. (name) is thoughtful, concerned, and compassionate in his dealings with his subordinates. In his position as supervisor, teacher, and counselor he displays the concerned compassion and professionalism of a model (peer group). He is actively involved in this command's retention team effort, and to enhance his effectiveness he requested and attended Career Counselor School. In addition to conducting group and one-on-one counseling sessions he has been active in setting up and conducting command-wide workshops that have received praise from all officers at this command.

4. A thorough review of (name) record substantiates the fact that his performance of excellence has continued throughout his Naval career. As revealed through personal letters of commendation and appreciation, it is quite apparent that he has continually devoted himself to the Navy through his knowledge and application of his professional tools.

5. (name) academic ability and progress are outstanding. He has completed ... semester hours of college credit at the University of ... with a grade point average of ... and has consistently graduated in the upper half of his class at service schools.

6. (name) is highly motivated toward a career in the Navy and for selection to commissioned status. In view of his continued display of loyalty, dedication, and reliability, he is considered an excellent candidate for appointment to (WO/LDO).

CWO - LDO ENDORSEMENT

SAMPLE #9

1. Forwarded, most strongly recommending approval.

2. (name) is intelligent, energetic, and innovative. Throughout his career he has consistently excelled in his rating and in a leadership capacity. His comprehensive technical knowledge, initiative, and leadership was aptly displayed during this command's (mission). (name) enthusiastic approach toward setting and achieving mission goals, and his natural flair for counseling significantly enhanced the performance of the (organization) department. Through his leadership, patience, and uniquely personalized instructional technique, many less than receptive personnel have been successfully motivated and inspired to work to the highest level of their ability. (name) has systematically planned and organized complex tasks, demonstrating superior managerial and supervisory abilities. His unparalleled proficiency in his technical specialty and in ... operations place him at the absolute forefront of his rate.

3. (name) strong technical background is the result of a long and diverse series of operational assignments. His experience base is broad and encompasses a wide range of professional specialties. Recognized as the resident authority in the knowledge of PMS, PQS, and damage

control as well as ... systems, (name) is consistently sought out for technical advice. His achievements in the technical aspects of his rate are vividly documented in his enlisted performance evaluation and testify to his thorough knowledge of his rate.

4. A concerned and humane individual, (name) affable personality and willingness to assist others in any capacity instills high morale and a strong sense of esprit de corps in those around him. Through personal industry and the effective use of correct management techniques he has shown that he can judiciously utilize personnel and material resources.

5. Dedicated to professional growth and personal self-development, (name) has methodically accumulated a record of academic accomplishments of unequalled magnitude. He has earned a Bachelor of Science Degree from the University of ..., and he has completed ... Navy correspondence courses and ... schools.

6. A proven performer of strong personal integrity and superb leadership and technical ability, (name) enjoys my absolute confidence that he will be an exceptional (WO/LDO). I would actively seek to have him assigned as a member of my wardroom, either ashore or afloat.

CWO - LDO ENDORSEMENT

SAMPLE #10

1. Forwarded, highly recommending approval.

2. (name) professional knowledge and technical competence is truly outstanding. He has fully demonstrated the strong leadership, exceptional management ability, and meticulous administrative skills that will enable him to discharge, in a superior manner, the broader duties and greater responsibilities of a (WO/LDO).

3. (name) professional performance has been consistently superior. He is currently serving as (billet) for the ... Department and has performed numerous division officer functions in this capacity. In all assignments, (name) has consistently performed his duties with skill, eagerness, ingenuity, and imagination, and he has been extremely effective in guiding assigned personnel in the performance of their duties. His personal contributions to command readiness and to mission effectiveness are well documented. He received a Navy Achievement Medal from ... for professional work and technical competence he displayed during (period). I personally awarded him a Letter of Commendation for his active and successful participation in ...

4. Evaluations received in well rounded duty assignments are evidence of (name) sustained superior performance and a strong desire to excel. His qualities of self-confidence, excellent physical condition, and commanding presence give him an unusual talent for the control of personnel. He maintains an impeccable personal appearance and commands similarly high standards from his subordinates, creating a deep respect for Navy tradition and regulations. He displays an understanding and an informed sense of judgement in his dealings with others, regardless of sex, race, or creed.

5. (name) has repeatedly demonstrated that he possesses those unique qualities of leadership and technical knowledge that identify him as truly outstanding and totally committed to excellence. (name) is highly recommended for selection to the (WO/LDO) Program.

CWO - LDO ENDORSEMENT

SAMPLE #11

1. Forwarded, strongly recommending approval.

2. (name) has thoroughly exhibited the potential to excel in the capacity of a (CWO/LDO). He is extremely dedicated and strongly motivated toward advancement within the Navy organization. Having clearly demonstrated consistent outstanding performance and potential in managerial and technical competence, (name) was personally selected to lead this command's ... program. His personal indepth knowledge and submitted resolutions to potential problems have been instrumental factors in the realized improvements to that program. During a Command Inspection conducted by TYCOM, the program was judged as the finest inspected in more than five years.

3. A meticulous administrator, (name) totally controlled all administrative matters in the department. Confronted with an error rate of 7% in the (area), (name) exercised strong supervisory control and promptly decreased the error rate to an impressive 2.1% within two months. This "take charge" administrative and leadership attitude does not end with his technical undertakings. He assumed the responsibility of coordinating the command's zone inspection program and produced equally impressive results. Additionally, these valuable traits and his managerial skills were instrumental in my appointing him to serve as Command ..., a demanding billet which he continues to serve in with unequalled distinction.

4. (name) is a well-rounded person of many interests. He continually takes positive steps to improve his knowledge and understanding of his technical field and in the world around him. He has completed eleven Navy schools and twenty-three correspondence courses. To date he has completed forty-eight semester hours of credit with the University of ..., and expects to earn his Associate Degree within the next year.

5. (name) exceptional technical knowledge, superb managerial abilities, and strong, positive leadership acquired through a series of challenging and diverse duty assignments combine in such a balanced manner as to stand him head and shoulders above his peers. No better candidate could be found for this program than this eager, mature, and dedicated Navy man. (name) is an ideal candidate for the (WO/LDO) Program.

6. (name) demonstrates, on a daily basis, that he is professionally and technically qualified for promotion to the Naval Officer Corps. He is strongly recommended for selection to commissioned status as (WO/LDO).

CWO - LDO ENDORSEMENT

SAMPLE #12

1.   Forwarded, highly recommending approval.

2.   (name) is a superb (WO/LDO) applicant in all respects. His military bearing, appearance, discipline, and moral character are of the highest order. He aggressively pursues difficult challenges and is tireless in his efforts to excel. Through successive tours on board ..., ..., and ..., (name) has experienced total diversity within his professional specialty of ... This experience combined with his extensive schooling provide and extraordinary high degree of technical knowledge.

3.   (name) organizational and managerial skills place him head and shoulders above his contemporaries. He is an exceptionally talented and versatile individual who has consistently achieved superior results in progressively more challenging assignments. His daily demonstrated extraordinary professional ability, in depth technical knowledge, and uncommon perceptiveness in advancing the morale and welfare needs of subordinates demonstrate unlimited growth potential. His desire and motivation to aspire to commissioned rank is refreshing. He is immediately capable of being promoted to (WO/LDO), and he has the spiritual force and moral fiber so necessary in a Naval leader. I am thoroughly convinced that (name) exemplifies those qualities and traits which merit his selection.

4. (name) has proven himself an excellent student in all Navy and civilian educational institutions. This education has provided him with diversified knowledge essential for an expanding Naval career.

5. The leadership and supervisory abilities (name) has demonstrated, coupled with his forthright confident manner, ensure his success in the officer community. He is extremely capable of accepting, and carrying out, the expanded responsibilities and increased trust associated with (WO/LDO).

6. Throughout his career, (name) has gained the prerequisite experience to excel as a (WO/LDO). The extraordinary manner in which he has managed his (organization) throughout his tour aboard provides vivid insight to his unlimited potential as a (WO/LDO). These strong traits coupled with his natural leadership abilities make (name) the best (specialty group) candidate for (WO/LDO) in the Navy.

CWO - LDO ENDORSEMENT

SAMPLE # 13

1. Forwarded, highly recommending approval.

2. (name) sets the standards in both military and professional performance. He stands head and shoulders above his contemporaries in all respects. His enthusiastic attitude, loyal dedication to the Naval service, and impressive accomplishments truly merit increased responsibility now.

3. (name) has firmly established himself as an outstanding leader whose performance and personal characteristics make him the epitome of what is desired in a Naval leader. His exceptional technical competence and supervisory ability are clearly evident in the outstanding results he achieves in all task assignments. He possesses the extra initiative, personal magnetism, moral fiber, patriotism and force which would make him a welcome addition to the officer corps of the United States Navy.

4. (name) has been a source of major administrative and operational contributions throughout his tour at this command. His innovative ideas in ... resulted in considerable savings of manhours for his department. One man was reassigned to a more important area of operation as a result of this savings. Additionally, he volunteered to conduct an extensive survey and assessment of ... system reliability. Following this survey he instituted a number of changes, including: updated ...; closer liaison between ... and ... personnel; and, a revitalized and updated quality control

testing acceptance program. To implement these sweeping changes, he followed-up with highly effective, expertly written, operating instructions and procedures, and a viable training program to ensure correct implementation. As a result of these extensive efforts, within six months ... system reliability increased from ... to ... percent. Recently, qualifying for designation as an Enlisted Surface Warfare Specialist, (name) became the first ever so designated from the ... Department.

5. As a military supervisor, (name) thrives on good personnel relationships through two-way communications with his subordinates and is effective in imparting to them the importance of this human element in the overall mission of the command. (name) deep and abiding personal concern for the welfare of others is not limited to work hours. He involves himself in as many community affairs as time permits and is an active and productive member of ... and ... (name) is a sober, responsible person who takes his home life very seriously and he maintains a highly stable family life.

6. (name) is a natural choice for selection to the (WO/LDO) Program and he has my highest recommendation.

CWO - LDO ENDORSEMENT

SAMPLE # 14

1. Forwarded, most strongly recommending approval.

2. (name) qualifications for the (WO/LDO) Program are without equal. While sustaining an extraordinary level of performance, he consistently demonstrates those qualities required in a (WO/LDO); exceptional technical knowledge, superb managerial capability, and strong positive leadership. His superior administrative abilities are known and respected throughout this command. As a leader, (name) successfully couples a strong positive drive for excellence with sincere concern for the welfare of each member of his organization.

3. (name) record is impressive. His career has followed a pattern of steady growth in technical skills and leadership. Since reporting aboard he has filled increasingly demanding billets with unparalleled success. A self-starter who thrives on challenge, he performed flawlessly while simultaneously filling eight primary and collateral duties, including ...

4. (name) need to improve himself personally and professionally is manifested in his intense desire to pursue both on and off duty educational goals. He has attended a variety of military and civilian educational institutions with consistently high academic performance. Working many extra hours at this command has not diminished this desire.

He has found time to complete five off-duty college courses, in a variety of technical and management subjects, while maintaining a grade-point average of ...

5.   (name) personal appearance, military bearing, and personal behavior are commendable. His sense of humor, mental alertness, and ability to express himself both orally and in writing is excellent. He is a sound manager with the proven ability to successfully supervise the functions and activities of others while maintaining, or surpassing, command objectives.

6.   It is without reservation or condition that I recommend (name) for (WO/LDO). I would particularly be pleased to have (name) as a member of my wardroom, either ashore or afloat.

CWO - LDO ENDORSEMENT

SAMPLE # 15

1. Forwarded, strongly recommending approval.

2. (name) is the most dynamic (peer group) that I have ever observed. His technical qualifications are absolutely first rate, and his experience qualifies him superbly to be a (WO/LDO) technical manager. Even more important, he is a "military professional" in the fullest sense of the term. He is a strong, positive leader who will be a credit to the officer corps. Without hesitation, I rank him number one of the four enlisted personnel in my command applying for the (WO/LDO) Program.

3. (name) seeks responsibility and is always ready to carry more than his share of the work load. Although quiet by nature, he enthusiastically and diligently pursues opportunities to enhance his career. He possesses the experience, leadership abilities, motivation, attitude, and loyalty required of a Naval Officer.

4. In his assignment as ..., (name) consistently performed his duties with skill, eagerness, ingenuity, and was extremely effective in guiding assigned personnel in the performance of their duties. His exceptional leadership skills and managerial abilities enabled him to train and develop a highly capable and productive team of professionals.

Under his tutelage and direction his shop became a model of excellence. Through his guidance non- productive maintenance was all but eliminated, resulting in substantial monetary savings to the command. His ability to recognize and document superior performance in others resulted in recognition of two of his personnel being selected as "Sailor of the Quarter" and in the awarding of NECs being earned by three men trained by him.

5. After only a short association with (name), it will become readily apparent that he is unswerving in his loyalty to the Navy and is steadfastly determined to accomplish any task in an outstanding manner. He maintains a stable family life, possesses high morals, and is intricately involved in numerous community activities.

6. (name) entire career shows strong self-motivation and a particularly desirable attitude towards the Navy. A proven manager who obtains results equal to or surpassing command objectives, he is an outstanding candidate for commissioned status as (WO/LDO).

7. (name) has my strongest possible recommendation for commission as (WO/LDO).

CWO - LDO ENDORSEMENT

SAMPLE # 16

1. Forwarded, highly recommending approval.

2. (name) is an exceptionally talented and well-qualified candidate who has consistently displayed superlative performance in a wide range of duties. His career pattern reflects steady growth in both technical and management skills. While serving at this command, he has performed three challenging and demanding billets requiring thorough knowledge of his rate and exemplary leadership. As (job), his responsibilities encompassed all aspects of ... He provided the expertise to maintain a consistent, smooth flowing operation, and ensured errorless (subject). (name) demonstrated maturity and outstanding knowledge of his technical specialty as Department (job). In his third job of Department (job), he was effective in reducing the error rate of ... system from ... to ... percent within the past year, thereby improving the operation of the ... Department and the creditability of this command.

3. (name) off-duty educational achievements are praiseworthy. He has successfully completed a variety of college level examination tests and night school classes, accumulating a total of ... semester hours of college credit. He is presently within ... hours of earning a BS in ... through the University of ... He has earned a place on the Dean's List for academic excellence during each of the last two years.

4.   (name) entire career shows strong self-motivation and a positive attitude toward the Navy. A proven manager who obtains results surpassing command objectives, he is an outstanding candidate for (WO/LDO).

5.   (name) is the caliber of Navy professional sought by the (WO/LDO) Program. His untiring dedication to the completion of tasks and the initiative he shows in improving conditions within his (organization) and his command have earned my respect and complete confidence in his abilities. (name) is unconditionally prepared and I strongly recommend him for selection as a (WO/LDO). I would be particularly pleased to have him as a member of my wardroom.

CWO - LDO ENDORSEMENT

SAMPLE # 17

1. Forwarded, highly recommending approval.

2. (name) possesses a well-rounded knowledge of his rate, both afloat and ashore. His attention to detail, foresight in planning, and organizational ability are superior in all respects and are demonstrated daily by his skillful direction of his work center. His counseling expertise, and the meticulous record keeping displayed in the performance of both his primary and collateral duties, are unequalled. His diverse background as ... operator, ... operator and supervisor, and training petty officer at such major commands as ... and ... have most certainly prepared him for the increased responsibility he seeks. This impressive experience coupled with the "can-do" attitude he consistently demonstrates is ready testimony to (name) potential ability to excel as an ... category (WO/LDO).

3. (name) unique ability to relate to personnel of varied age groups and backgrounds is enhanced by his use of candor, tact, and diplomacy when dealing with them on a personal basis. This, plus the wisdom that comes with years of experience, makes him an extremely effective counselor. His promotion of fair and equal treatment is openly evident to juniors, peers, and seniors alike. Each person is given assignments commensurate with ability and all are afforded the opportunity to advance.

4.　(name) possesses the leadership qualities and the administrative, organizational, and professional abilities to perform well as an officer. He is considered an outstanding candidate for commissioning as a ... category (WO/LDO).

5.　(name) is highly recommended for promotion to (WO/LDO). I would seek his services as an officer now or in the future.

CWO - LDO ENDORSEMENT

SAMPLE # 18

1.   Forwarded, highly recommending approval.

2.   (name) has been an outstanding (peer group) at this command. He is a self assured individual who can be relied upon to complete any task assigned to him. His management ability was first evidenced when he was assigned the billet of ..., a demanding billet normally held by (pay grade). (name) performed exceptionally well in this assignment. He regarded his new duties as presenting an opportunity to further his growth in the Navy, typifying the enthusiasm and attitude that he has demonstrated throughout his tour at this command.

3.   (name) proven supervisory ability, organization aptitude and constant daily awareness of operational requirements are above reproach. His knowledge of logistics, material, and personnel, and his ability to comprehend task requirements are indicative of his readiness for increased responsibility as an ... officer.

4.   Human values are extremely important to (name). Accordingly, he is a model promoter of fair play and equal treatment. His tactful, but firm, manner of associating with subordinates and peers clearly indicate that he is a "people person" with the ability to meet all operational tasking. He

ensures the job is completed correctly and on time, and that all subordinates are given an equal opportunity to contribute. His written reports are clear, concise, and require virtually no editing before being forwarded to superiors.

5. (name) ability to perform in an academic setting can easily be seen by his record of accomplishment in Navy schools, correspondence courses, and through off-duty education with ... College. Possessed of keen and disciplined mind, his study selections show the desire to expand and grow in both professional and military matters, as well as in human behavior studies and administrative skills.

6. (name) flawless military demeanor and conduct are in keeping with his other superior traits. He possesses all of the attributes most desired of an officer candidate. (name) is highly recommended for promotion to (WO/LDO).

CWO - LDO ENDORSEMENT

SAMPLE #19

1. Forwarded, highly recommending approval.

2. (name) has performed all military and professional duties in a manner second to none. He has demonstrated the ability to build and maintain an excellent working organization that has gained the cooperation and support of juniors and seniors alike. (name) is an ardent achiever who welcomes responsibilities and completes each assignment to the best of his ability. No task is too menial or arduous.

3. (name) is an exceptionally talented and versatile (peer group) who has consistently achieved superior results in progressively more challenging assignments. While serving as (job), he displayed both exceptional management skill and thorough technical knowledge. As a result of actions he implemented, operators were afforded a more flexible working environment which improved the responsiveness of his area of responsibility. Concurrently, his emphasis on training and organizational procedures improved operating efficiency to the point the ... percent manning posture impacted little on overall division effectiveness. Through careful attention to sound management principles, he effected a ... percent reduction in the division budget, accruing a ... dollar savings to the command. In recognition of his outstanding performance, he

was subsequently appointed as (job), a billet normally assigned to a (pay grade). In this job, he is again demonstrating his strong performance in operational, fiscal, and personnel management.

4. (name) total dedication to the Naval service, coupled with well-developed professional, leadership, and management skills make him an excellent choice for selection as a Naval Officer. Employing effective and positive communications to present ideas with power and persuasion, (name) logically communicates goals and interplay of ideas and concepts. Accordingly, (name) professional capability and dynamic approach to his job impart a sense of pride, motivation, and initiative in all those with whom he is associated.

5. (name) is more than ready to assume the increased leadership role of a Naval Officer. He is an ideal candidate and is highly recommended for (WO/LDO).

CWO - LDO ENDORSEMENT

SAMPLE # 20

1. Forwarded, highly recommending approval.

2. (name) is a highly qualified (WO/LDO) candidate. He continually demonstrates exceptional resourcefulness and professionalism as (job). He exhibits superb managerial skills and high personal initiative in a relentless pursuit of perfection in meeting his daily commitments. (name) is a model supervisor. He has only to recognize a need to initiate action to eliminate that need. His tactful and sincere manner in dealing with subordinates secures their loyalty and inspires them to strive to reach the highest possible level of achievement. He is poised, confident, and composed at all times. In carrying out his duties as ..., he applied his past experience and training to make significant improvements in ... procedures and equipment operation. As a result, the ... Division regularly meets or exceeds established standards for ... Concurrently, he devised and implemented improved procedures and instituted enhanced operator training in systems/equipment operation and quality control which have measurably improved division operations.

3.   (name) continually strives to increase his knowledge and flexibility. His off duty study includes managerial and professionally oriented courses. In his area of technical expertise, he continually seeks additional responsibility and is ready to give advise and guidance to subordinates when the need arises. (name) speaking and writing ability is far above that normally expected of personnel of his pay grade. His correspondence drafts and reports require virtually no editing prior to forwarding to higher authority.

4.   In summary, (name) has successfully accepted the challenging and demanding responsibilities of leadership and management in today's Navy. His performance established new standards of professional and military achievement for his contemporaries. When considering his rapid advancement to (rate), it is apparent that his accomplishments were a testimony to his creativeness, adaptability, charisma, and overall superior performance. He is highly motivated and eminently qualified for commission as a United States Naval Officer. It is with pride and confidence that I recommend (name) for appointment to (WO/LDO).

CWO - LDO ENDORSEMENT

SAMPLE # 21

1. Forwarded, strongly recommending approval.

2. (name) is a sterling example of a fine (peer group), demonstrating outstanding potential for additional responsibility. He is strongly recommended for this program, and I would be most pleased to have him serve in my command as a (WO/LDO).

3. (name) is eminently qualified for the (WO/LDO) Program. He is a dedicated professional who thrives on new challenges. He is an extraordinary supervisor, highly competent in any endeavor. He invariably improves all facets of his area of responsibility and considers efficiency in all jobs to be a matter of routine. His performance is consistently outstanding as (job) and he attains brilliant performance from subordinates. His supervisory skills are extraordinary. Despite a constant personnel turnover inherent in division operations, he maintains a smooth-running unit which exceeds all production quotas without sacrificing quality. (name) charismatic personality has greatly enhanced not only his team's morale, but also that of the entire division.

4. (name) intense desire for self improvement is evidenced in his steady pursuit of a college degree. He has accumulated ... semester hours of college credit and is currently preparing for the CLEP general examinations which will result in completing the requirements for an Associates Degree. His advanced education enables him to easily interpret official directives, technical instructions, and publications. More importantly, he applies the knowledge gained from his learning experience in a most practical and highly productive manner.

5. I consider (name) to be one of the finest (peer group) in my command. He is a superb candidate and is fully capable of handling the increased responsibilities of a (WO/LDO). He is a highly responsible and loyal career man who is dedicated to contributing his best to service and country. His performance, leadership, conduct, and appearance excel. (name) is eminently qualified and I strongly recommend him for a commission as a (WO/LDO).

CWO - LDO ENDORSEMENT

SAMPLE # 22

1. Forwarded, highly recommending approval.

2. (name) displays an ideal mix of professional, military, intellectual, and leadership capabilities and abilities which mark him as an exceptional candidate for the (WO/LDO) Program in the field of ...

3. (name) has a strong desire to serve as a (WO/LDO). An extraordinary individual who relishes a demanding pace and intense workload, (name) is an inspirational leader who instills pride in his assigned personnel by setting and achieving extremely high standards of performance. Accordingly, he has the greatest possible confidence in his ability to serve as a (WO/LDO).

4. (name) was initially assigned duties of ... in the ... Department. His performance in that capacity was exceptional and he was subsequently assigned duties as ... because of his dynamic leadership and overall superb performance. In this new position, he has maintained his outstanding personal performance in technical areas and has initiated positive action to improve the military and professional performance of assigned personnel. He is again proving that strong leadership makes the decisive difference in overcoming problems of aging equipment, personal turbulence, and marginal logistics support.

5.   (name) devoted the majority of his off-duty time to correcting the problems he inherited with his assignments at work. However, as his efforts realized improved equipment reliability and his off-duty time became more his own, he became involved in conducting Sunday School classes for children. He is also an active member of the ... Club, and Secretary of the ... Association.

6.   (name) is fully qualified in all respects and will perform extremely well as a (WO/LDO) in the ... area. He possesses the mental dexterity and technical competence to become an excellent (WO/LDO). He has earned my unqualified endorsement for promotion to officer status under this program.

THIS PAGE LEFT BLANK FOR YOUR NOTES

CHAPTER

NINE

MAINTAIN

YOUR OWN

BRAG

SHEET

CHAPTER 9

BRAG SHEET

This short chapter is perhaps the most important chapter in this writing guide for you personally.

A comment was made earlier in this guide to the effect that "If you don't know how to write a performance appraisal, you don't know how to read one--your own included."

Unfortunately, most people being evaluated don't learn the real difference between a good, strong write-up and one that "sounds" good until it is too late in their career to do much good. Because of rank, position, or education, many "khakis" falsely believe that they are automatically good performance appraisal writers. As a result of this false assumption, they hurt themselves and the good performers who work for them. A "sounds good" narrative is as much your fault as it is the person who writes it--you let him do it to you. A good write-up must have some substance, some job accomplishment specifics.

Regardless of how you end up with a "low," say-nothing narrative, if you are a good performer it is your fault and you are the one who is going to be "passed over" at selection time.

Everyone has an opportunity to submit information they would like to have considered when performance appraisal time comes around. For example, if you submitted an input that contained the following facts, your superiors would be hard-pressed to not use the information in your narrative.

-Qualified DC PQS in 2 months, one-third the normal time.

-Completed 3 correspondence courses.

-Qualified OOD (Inport) in 3 weeks, 4 months ahead of schedule.

-Initiated watch station PQS standards for 4 work groups totaling 25 people. Standards were approved and implemented.

-Worked 75 off-duty hours drafting and finalizing a Division Organization Manual.

-Assigned personnel received "OUTSTANDING" at 3 department and 2 command personnel inspections.

The list could go on and on. The point is **THERE IS A LIST**. Commit yourself to maintaining a "brag sheet" file throughout a reporting period. If you don't come up with two or three items a week to place in the file, you aren't trying--or you aren't doing your job.

When it is time to provide an input to your performance appraisal, break out everything you have, compile it and then decide what you want to use.

Keep in mind, your superiors probably don't have the time to record all of the accomplishments of everyone who works for them. For a top performer, they would be happy to include any important information you submit. Plus, providing this information makes a superior's job of constructing a narrative much easier.

The more information you have in your brag file the better. Include dates, hours worked, and any other information needed to give specific accomplishments and tasks.

The following items are offered to get you started. Add to it items particular or unique to your job or billet. These items could be appropriate to you individually, or to your work group.

1. Reenlistment (numbers/percentages).

2. Advancement (numbers/percentages).

3. PQS (military/professional) completed.

4. Correspondence courses.

5. Off-duty education.

6.Inspection results: zone...material...security...command... safety...administrative...personnel.... berthing/barracks...type training... 3M...retention team...

7. Graded exercises.

8. Financial budget (save $).

9. Organization manning allowance/onboard/onboard percent.

10. Average work-week hours.

11. Accomplishments/Distinctions received by department/command (and what you did to help).

12. Organization correspondence forwarded correct/timely.

13. What your organization did to help meet command objectives and commitments.

14. Special/Additional assistance given others (individuals or organizations).

15. New programs you had a hand in starting.

16. Improvements to spaces/working conditions.

17. Directives, SOPs, instructions originated/ up-dated.

18. Command and community involvement.

19. Collateral duties (volunteer for many): Navy Relief Key Person, CFC Key Person, Welfare & Recreation... This list is almost endless. Volunteer for several. Many require only a few hours a month/year, and the rewards are well worth the effort.

20. Major evolutions participated in.

21. Extra hours worked.

22. Extra projects worked on (outside normal area of responsibility or outside normal working hours).

Look through the listing on the previous pages and you can get some more ideas. A good way to meet this challenge would be to go over a long list of possible "achievements," pick out the ones you like best, and go and do them--and then make additions to your brag file. Again, it's your write-up; it's your future...Leave no stone unturned.